Tocayo

Also by Joe Doerr

Order of the Ordinary

(as Editor)
The Salt Companion to John Matthias

Joe Doerr

Tocayo

New & Selected
Poems & Songs

Shearsman Books

First published in the United Kingdom in 2016 by
Shearsman Books
50 Westons Hill Drive
Emersons Green
BRISTOL
BS16 7DF

Shearsman Books Ltd Registered Office
30–31 St. James Place, Mangotsfield, Bristol BS16 9JB
(this address not for correspondence)

www.shearsman.com

ISBN 978-1-84861-471-0

CONTENTS

LOVE FAVORS THE PRODIGAL:
NEW POEMS FOR THE SAGE & SAVAGE

Tocayo	13
The Catch	17
The Driven	20
I. Hill	20
II. Peck	20
III. Smith	21
While You're Out Remember	22
The Kings of Cryptomnesia	23
Pax Animalia	25
1: The Judas Goat	25
2: The Koomkie	25
3: The Stale Pigeon	26
Diptych: Drapetomania	27
I. Di[agnosis]	27
II. "Der" Lehrer to the 21st C. Drapetomaniac	28
The Cottage Wall	29
[Byron's Pistols]	29
[A Minority of One]	29
[The Revolvita]	30
[The Minstrel Boy]	31
[The Merchant of Menace]	31
[Il Miglior Mirare]	32
[Belly of the Whale]	32
[William, Do Tell]	33
[The Rumored Boss]	34
[A Barbarian Explains Himself]	34
[Billy in the Box]	35
[He Carries the Fire]	36
St. Louis Gothic	37
Sestina: Querencia	39
To the Dryad in Her Eightieth Year	41
In Nomine Something	42

Nine Twenty-Four Times Nine: A Clutch of Birthday Poems 44
  [Il Faut Aller Voir] 44
  [Geronimo] 45
  [A Disambiguation in the Garden] 46
  [September Moon] 47
  [Anagram: "Sonnet 18"] 48
  [Choice Un-chosen] 48
  [Queen of the Fisher Kings] 49
  [The Dig] 50
  [Remember Me] 51

REPETITIO EST FILIAM OBLITUS LIBRO: SELECTED POEMS FOR THEM WHAT BLINKED

Epistolary Suite: Three Letters for Friends Gone Missing 55
  [Thou Philip, Thief of Loco-Focos] 55
  [Anderson, The Snow Flies] 57
  [On the State of Disunion, Inter Alia] 63
Letters to Woodhenge 67
  [Why the Earth Shakes] 67
  [Introit] 68
  [Notes & Conversations] 68
  [Backtracking] 69
  [Kyrie] 69
  [Aus-Tex Proceeds from Cahokia] 69
  [Joplin] 70
  [Gloria] 70
  [Mythissippi Mud] 71
  [A Handful of Dust] 71
  [Credo] 72
  [Saarinen] 72
  [Burroughs] 73
  [Offertory] 74
  [Swimming Near the Guardrail] 74
  [January Thaw] 75
  [Sanctus] 75
  [James Arthur Defenestrates Winter] 75
  [The Delta Queen in Dire Straits] 76

[Agnus Dei]   76
[Brubeck Serenades the Snow Queen]   77
[Desmond Takes Five from Dying]   77
[Communion]   78
[Desmond & the Piasa Bird]   78
[Star-crossed]   79
[Benedicamus]   79
[AN. I ^M. DCCCCXCVII. Her Æteowde
             Se Feaxede Steorra]   79
Futhark 2K   81
[feoh] Wealth   81
[ur] The Wild Ox   81
[thorn] The Thorn   81
[ansuz] Language   82
[rad] Riding   82
[cen] The Torch   83
[gyfu] The Gift   83
[wyn] Joy   83
[hægl] Hail   84
[nyd] Need   84
[is] Ice   84
[ger] The Year   85
[eoh] The Yew   85
[peorth] The Game   86
[eolhxsecg] Marsh Grass   86
[sigel] The Sun   86
[tir] A Star   87
[beorc] The Birch   87
[eh] The Horse   87
[man] The Human Being   88
[lagu] The Sea   88
[ing] The God of Fertility   89
[ethel] Native Land   89
[dæg] The Day   89
[ac] The Oak   90
[æsc] The Ash   90
[yr] The Bow   90
[iar] A Sea Creature   91
[ear] The Clay   91
[…] The Unknowable   92

The Chord   93
Thumbnails For a Portrait of Sacher-Masoch   98
    I   Die Kunst des Jägers   98
    II   Die Kunst des Bauers   98
    III   Die Kunst des Ölmalers   99
    IV   Die Kunst der Heilerin   99
Sestina for the Birds   101

UNACCOMPANIED: SONGS FOR DISTANT MUSIC

Pontiac Flanagan   105
Rimbaud Diddley   106
Vendidi Fumar (I Sell Smoke)   107
Melungeon in the Dungeon   109
Supermonisticgnostiphistic   111
Pity the Noose   112
Can O'Worms   113
Metanoia   114
Rickshaw Rattletrap   115
Ulysses   118
Abraxas   119
Aranzazu   121
Money Shot Man   122
Fake This One   124
Duende   125
Weedeye   126
A Message from Firmin Desloge   128
You Be the Mountain (I'll Be Mohammad)   129
Keels Be Damned   130
Cain   132
Shake the Vine   133
Holla Petunia   135
Éminence Gris Gris   136
I Spit You Out   137
Drapetomaniac   139
Hystery Train   140
Chemtrailer Trash   141
Triptych   142

AFTERWARD:
ONE FOR THE MEMORIES

Mem[ory]sahib   145

Notes   146
Acknowledgments   148

for my mother,
who always insisted that I draw my own tree
i.m. (1927-2015)

Love Favors the Prodigal:

New Poems

FOR THE SAGE & SAVAGE

Tocayo

Come, all ye tribes of serpents and foul fish!
Beetle and worm, I have a feast for you!
          —Aleister Crowley

The first strains of *Tannhäuser* made by a Sawzall —
Specifically B/E/B/G# — before
Ascending into approximations of whale song,
Ground their way through a stubborn length of rebar
On that *Miércoles de Ceniza* —
                              Consequently I
Rejoice[d], having to construct something upon
Which to rejoice when the Roach Coach's wheels
Came crunching through the damp *caliche*
Abaft of its breakfast-announcing cuminous stench.

Toting a plate of beans and chorizo, my coffee
Lightened by unsweetened milk, and a centipede
Curious about the gray flecks on my boot heel,
I commandeered a stack of 2x4s and sat
Anxious not for company, but for morning solitude.

But he sat too, having first asked permission,
His coastal Texas accent flat and green and smooth,
Though his features gave the lie to all of this and more.

The Rastafarian tam of Garvey colors—
Red, black, green, and yellow bands of wool—
Worn Pericles high and pushed off the brow line,
Made him seem less politic than refined.

He called me *tocayo*, shook hands as *Joseph*,
Talked of carpentry, women, Melville, and time.

The last he claimed to be done with killing;
Having done it had smothered his yen to hang fire.
And murder, to which he no longer cottoned,
Was anathematic to his new moral code.

I'd heard the rumors; he was no angel,
An anti-*santo* and apoca-prophet, yes,
But one whose company was the picture of peace.

Prior to the prolix yarn of his conviction and sentence,
He had made it his business to furnish the dead:
Great slabs of purple heartwood,
Spalted tamarind, wengé, and mun
Became in his hands the bedsteads of the breathless,
Terminal fixtures for those whinnying with us not.

He'd made a simple living, so he claimed,
And called it *Queequeg's Coffin,*
Selling to those who wanted something
Uniquely final, or finally unique.

He'd made his own as well; or rather,
Made one for himself—it was carefully worked
Of Yaje and Cocobolo in the classic coffin shape:
An elongated hexagram with a simple sliding lid

On which he'd carved a personal charm:
A white rose blooming from a thorn-encrusted cane.

When finished, he'd placed it in the attic hollow,
A space above his living place of rest—
The bed he shared with a woman who'd betray him—
Ready to receive him,
                         ready there and waiting for his time.

Impassioned men are prone to crimes of passion,
And by some trick of nature find it difficult to bear
The same propensity for passion found in others—
Or such was Joseph's theory;
and as theories go, it's fair.
He'd killed the man who for a time at least
Had lain beneath his coffin; had lain beneath,
Above perhaps, the woman he desired;

Had come, at any rate, between
Two objects of his passion—his words, not mine.

Fifteen years of punish and appeal,
Fifteen years of contemplating time,
Fifteen years of books and conversations
Had placed something like redemption in his grasp.

The woman who'd betrayed him never gave up
In her efforts to secure him an appeal,
To secure him his release.

She'd worked three jobs
                                    and went through all her savings;
Lawyer after lawyer threw his hands up in defeat,
Till one agreed to take the case
For a most unusual fee,

And managed to make a fine appeal
Before a sympathetic judge.

The sentence was reduced to time served—Joseph
Had no idea who had been responsible for this.

The day he was released he saw her standing
Near the entrance, near the exit, nearly frantic in her joy.
She embraced him, he forgave her,
                                    they remembered who they were.

After the marathon making up,
                                    and over a bottle of wine,

He'd asked her how she'd paid for such
A brilliant, young attorney who had argued
His appeal with success.

Your coffin
she had answered
it brought you back to me.

My coffin
he kept saying
it took me back to her.

The coffin
I repeated
it raised you from the dead.

—para mi tocayo

The Catch

A heron's rasping call from somewhere
higher than dusk
settling in the canopy of cottonwood
sounding desperate
as it echoes through the creek bed.

The men appear from downstream,
two of them,
in cotton shirts and cut-offs,
cautiously wading
from the deep pools to the sandbar.

Along this stretch of arroyo
the high banks surrender
to suburban lawns of Bermuda,

St. Augustine and Buffalo
            sprawling from the edges of patios
                  their exotic flora trim
                        by contrast to the tangle

of beggarstick and broomsedge,
bristlejoint and chess

where I stand drinking,
a guest in a backyard
not my own,
one eye open
for arrowheads in the chirt
as the last minutes of daylight turn blue.

Hola,
and all at once
three hands are raised in greeting;
all eyes present
narrow with suspicion
of the other,

posture is contagious,
growing mannish and compressed.

Then distance
between us narrows
and soon we are speaking.

punta de flecha
vino
canto del garza
mi hogar

It is revealed
the men have traveled to this city
to find work
quite unlike the work
they knew as other men
in a distant village by the sea.

It is revealed
the men long for homes
that are no longer,
for connections with a past
that has all but passed away.

It is revealed
the men are fishing
with homemade nets and anchors,

and if one were so inclined
to use the language of the courts,
the men are poachers

who worry that I
or someone who is not me
will choose to use such language
to reveal them tonight.

*   *   *

A heron's rasping cry from somewhere
higher than the darkness
now settled in the canopy of sky
sounding desperate

       as I walk up from the creek bed
            to the lawn.
                    Then something more:

¡Señor!, they whisper, *¡Señor!*
¡A ver nuestra pesca!

The Driven

I. Hill

Not quite the hushed Vosges it led to,
that road from South Bend Regional.

Not quite the enemy's country, either,
though Old Blue Eyes' own 'September Song'
would penetrate the static of an FM station,
declare war on the gravity of expectation,
and mock conspiratorially with the catch
beneath the shotgun seat
     where Offa's shadow rode.

Not a proper taxi—preposterous that hatchback,
ridiculous in dimension—my circus miniscule,
all the more outrageous
     for its inconvenient flaw:

I hit the brakes and the prof slides forward;
I press the gas and the good knight shuttles fro.

II. Peck

The last train departed Union Station,
South Bend in 1971.
None of us knew that in the year of *M
and Other Poems*; all of us strangers in town,
we circled W. South in our golden ratio,
not quite unaware or unawares—
   "*What is the sign in you of your maker?
/* We are to say, *It is movement and repose.*"

The man who speaks of primordial imagery speaks
with a thousand tongues—and if by pondering signs

he misses, yes, his train perhaps he catches
something other: *Did you see that homeless
guy? I think he was a Mexican; the spiral
on his poncho was hypnotic. Hypnotic.*

III. Smith

"My gentle mother's furious resolve."
The Fox held the line with his tongue running
circles round its contours before he broke it
and the silence in the car the way Leopold
Bloom might break an egg against his palate.

I, pleased he'd found my poem worthy
of recitation, steered him to another bit
of manuscript I felt he might enjoy.

He'd an empty styrofoam cup he held aloft —
Where—?
      The floor is fine, I offered,
              and he chuckled:

*I rode once with Robert Bly who'd
brought along a fast-food meal;*

*the wrappings he kicked beneath the seat. Christ,
I told him, some Iron John you are.*

While You're Out Remember

Don't stop in Canning Town,
the pub's shut and the lift's out
in the towerblock.
Don't lose your head in Plaistow.

Move on till you're
one stop short of Barking
in a room above the garden
in a haze of vodka and orange,
a little weed and jet lag.

Settle on these stones:
try the eyeholes of a death mask,
finger the broken church glass
just this side of the border—
linger, longer if you want.

All the guests of this Republic
of Bad Manners come to shed
themselves of burdens, lives unlived.

We vie for the place of honor
in the corner by the loo.
We laugh and love and leave.

And tomorrow
Theydon Bois and all its ghosts
will find us limping
up that hill
where we ditched that branch of yew
that had served us all that day.

—i.m. Ken Smith (1938-2003)

The Kings of Cryptomnesia

Bread-breakers they might have called us
in that kingdom Auden dreamed of—
amniotic and diplopic;
Edenesque without the bother,
or fear of the enemy's purview.

I see us there in easy nescience
of any postlapsarian fix;
companions or compadres,
Mediterranean by way of Åsgård,
surely; primitively Roman,
catholic in some linear sense;
monarchic, even, if it be *She* who rules
our sharing of this vintage—

Ε πιθι ε απιθι—

Quaff or piss off!
the tag on the black dog's collar reads
here in your parlor Gethsemene,
where the influence of anxiety hangs
like the smoke of benedictions
blown through the Altamiras of the skull.

Full of sacrifice
and sated on her wine,
we will conjure the flint-knappers
who first let stones wound
and lead them as they labored
to release the shapes within.

And then the ghosts
who've left their marks in paint
and powdered ochre blown
through reed and ulna,
twig and bone,
and ask them to intercede—
for the next stop is the written word.

Ask them, these fathers,
these mothers whom we've never known,
to imbue and forgive, ask them to inspire.
Ask them to work new frescoes here,
to labor by the light of Aphelion
caught in a wick of juniper.

Ask them to find the shape in the rock
and asseverate there is but one message
bound by the order of design.

And in those Altamiras never
in the least bit bound
by the limits of the temple,
we at the edges of ceremony
who listen to the rite
through a chink in the crumbling wall
transcribe in our capacity
as kings of cryptomnesia
the evident liturgy of the endless and ailing world.

—for John Matthias

Pax Animalia

1: [The Judas Goat]

Huddling in trepidation of the piss stench,
the unseen limit of the pasture's lea,
sprayed round the perimeter in pulsing arcs
from a hand-held plastic pump can,
the flock cares nothing of the shepherd's plot.

It moves as one and nears the outmost building,
the faintly iron stink it takes for care:
wolf bleeds, coyote spills his innards, fox dies,
but ram and ewe and lamb will never need.

Chute funnel narrows, the bleating betters edgy—
the circle closes tightly till the Judas goat appears.

His scent is feed and rutting, and his confidence is clear;
there in the huddle, his kiss has gone viral:
he enters the shambles, the others follow suit.

2: [The Koomkie]

Fleeing the bonfires and scores of wooden clappers,
the frightened scramble belies the word *parade*—
or *keddah*, as the place demands—and seeks an entrance
to the jungle; tricked, it finds instead
                              the grim stockade.

Forty feet above, The Prince huddles
on his grass-roofed platform, pleased to see
fierce struggles from the fugitives below. The *koomkies*
enter, and though reviled unmistakably

by their jungle brethren, drive the wild
tuskers to the designated spot, where *khurus*
armed with torches urge their captives on.

Trumpeting through this bottleneck of branches,
the mammoths deadlock in a sealed cul-de-sac.
Once broken, they are sold at auction.

3: [The Stale Pigeon]

A hut of boughs and timber to lure the salting,
by which the stale pigeon has been fixed.
The abattoir disguised: an old brush arbor
to the bird's eye—bull's eye to the hidden snare.

Seen well after it is heard, its sonic approach
is a carousel of noise: armies of bell-laden horses
crossing dense woods ahead of thunder;
the flock descends in ignorance to its end.

Passenger pigeon oil flows like butter
in the churn, following a harvest of hat feathers.

One recalls the wag from Woodstock c. 1830
who offered for sale "Wild birds domesticated
& stool pigeons trained to catch voters for the next
Presidency—warranted to suit either party."

Diptych: Drapetomania

I. Di[agnosis]

"In noticing a disease not heretofore classed among the long list of maladies that man is subject to, it was necessary to have a new term to express it."
—Samuel A. Cartwright, 'Report on the Diseases and Physical Peculiarities of the Negro Race' (1851)

To know for certain whether Dr. Cartwright
could smell the lie in his own ersatz conclusions,
would be to know the color of despair.

Was he simply cozy with the sepulcher washed white?
Or a paradox addled by the state of his own affairs?

Freedom was a devil whose minions needed beating:
when paternalism failed, it was best to raise contusions,

then justify such perfidy with invention and deceiving.

δραπετης + μανια (the madness of a runaway slave)—
how elegantly pseudo and how classically designed,

this "newly identified," heretofore "unrecognized"
"disorder" particular to the peculiar institution.

But pseudo is yet honored in the house of retribution,
and madness wasn't buried with Cartwright in his grave.

II. "Der" Lehrer to the 21st C. Drapetomaniac

"This is how they reacted to the dissonance of being wrong: by becoming even more certain that they were right."
　　　—Jonah Lehrer, *The Psychology of Conspiracy Theories* (2010)

Go on—worry; question; be skeptical; try
to jam the gears of this unthinkable world,
then shuffle up—receive the host of diagnoses:

This one salts the earth of unbridled tongues;
that one reins in the galloping fertility of "Why?";
all replace good doubt with "cognitive dissonance."

To stray from this is illness; it rights no wrongs.
Submit to the yoke and the master anamnesis.
Empiricism is of no concern when reality is gnarled
caringly, preemptively by those who dictate "truth."

Suspicion of doublespeak has been designated "faith,"
and deserves the derision now reserved for dissidents.

To yearn for independence is to demonstrate disorder:
profound psychosis, lunacy, a tendency to martyr.

The Cottage Wall

[Byron's Pistols]

The Lord slept in relative discomfort,
loaded pistols by his bed;
the breath and tears and tortures of his dreams
propped imperiously, as the sword-cane
he'd lost in Lake Geneva
had once leaned, beside his prosthetic shoe.

Leopold Becher of Saxony wrought
the .38-bore matched pair—
Bohemian flintlocks chased with horsemen
riding down a Turk in wooded landscape—
that could have been used for more
than shooting at empty brandy bottles.

Had Tom Moore's challenge been leveled in time
to avenge such fractious words
("leadless pistol," "evaporated balls"),
they might have scored where another's failed—or,
maybe fever's dismal claim
should have been trumped by a death more fitting.

[A Minority of One]

He is carrying a beautiful brand-
new double-barreled pistol,
and superb, no-less-immaculate
yellow leather cartridge case. "I've just fired
a shot," he says, then hollers,
"We must go gun down General Aupick."

Aupick had bedded Baudelaire's mother
widow of François (*son père*),

two decades earlier when young Charles
was but seven, a mere *bourgeon du mal*.
At twenty-seven, stolen
gun in hand, he climbs the walls between worlds.

Aupick, of course, is everything conquest:
flat, repackaged status quo.
Baudelaire is all urgency and fire
baiting fire—*Perrin Le Page à Paris*,
short one .60 caliber,
had never been so hot until that day.

[The Revolvita]

The Belgian "Vigilant American"
of eighteen seventy-three's
a good candidate: six shots, cheap enough,
seven-millimeter rounds—Lord knows
what brand of poetic justice
Arthur's wrist bore like the 8th wound of Christ.

The police reports and depositions
are vague with facts: "pistolet,"
as if the magic words had been blown out,
replaced with icy anger and revenge.
Each once joined in confluence,
now ox-bowed by the suppurating stream.

Rimbaud dreamed of meeting Billy the Kid,
of notching grips together
in the haunted wilds of New Mexico.
Verlaine's misaim bled nightmares in the pillows:
Harrar of horror's angels,
dark transactions, whole caravans of pain.

[The Minstrel Boy]

Diminutive he may have been; so small,
in fact, that Tom Jefferson
on meeting him mistook him for a child.
Perhaps this slight led to Moore's great dislike
of most things American;
chiefly, Democratic-Republicans.

They could champion freedom and yet defend
peculiar institutions
in the same breath, as long as breath was free.
Moore's songs would "never sound in slavery";
though critics said they *were* slaves
to that which doggerel had to offer.

His Irish up, the gauntlet down, he dared
to duel with Francis Jeffrey,
his arch-detractor, to whom t'was rumored,
empty pistols had been given—no shots
exchanged that day, for the law intervened
and hauled both off to face a common future.

[The Merchant of Menace]

"...[A]fter a violent altercation
with those pathetic peasants...,"
he writes his mother (1885)
that he'd left Aden; Ethiopia
seemed a likely conclusion
to prescient lines like "*J'aimais le désert.*"

Several thousand rifles were on their way
to him from France and Russia—
Nagants, Berdans (both I & II), even
lever-action Winchesters from the States—
"I will drive a caravan;
Je vais vendre ces armes à Ménélik."

As rank hyenas, ritually fed,
laughed near the gates of Harrar,
moonbeam & lantern lit his gilded pass—
Abdo Rinbo Shall Not Be Molested—
and something more in his belt:
a Colt "Thunderer" just like William Bonney's.

[Il Miglior Mirare]

"Guns: Oh Yes?" in the *New English Weekly*
(1933) ol' Ez
describes *Il Duce* as preventing war;
keeping "British-bank-owned-and-gun-run press"
and "bourgeois demo-liberal"
pipe-dreams from becoming more, as it were.

In a letter to Hemingway, he wrote:
"the buggers back of the bank
of Paris are more worth killin' than cats
that ain't got no guns to shoot back with, you
god damn lionhunter—why
not take a crack at 'em in their *wallet?*"

Like Hem, the 13-year-old Pound could shoot.
Cheltenham Military
Academy had made him a marksman
with Springfields and Krag-Jørgensen rifles.
Later, taking aim at the school, he'd write
he "could stand everything but the drilling."

[Belly of the Whale]

"That rifle on the wall of the labourer's
cottage or working-class
flat is the symbol of democracy.

It is our job to see that it stays there."
Blair's *Evening Standard* op-ed
chagrined ol' Blimp's "make believe democrats"

who felt moral superiority
was all one ever needed
to convince two wolves discussing dinner
with a sheep that mutton ought to vanish
from any future menus.
Were the tables turned, would wolves go hungry?

Auden's thoughts of "necessary murder"
lent credence to Orwell's fears:
"Majority rules!"—a meme as fascist
as any INGSOC government slogan.
"A simple weapon gives claws
to the weak [and pause to that majority]."

[William, Do Tell]

Authoritarians have a good time
playing their broken records
for anyone finding value in the quote.

He was an atheist junkie, a queer!
You'd have hated each other!
He shot his wife in Mexico playing
William Tell—ad nauseam.

Ad hominem jabs are sure to follow;
as though best to encourage
divisiveness along so-called "party lines";
as though resisting "a society
where the only [ones] allowed
to own guns are the [cops] & military"

were tantamount to being a fascist.
Senator "turn-them-all-in-

Mr.-and-Mrs.-America" Di
Feinstein carried a concealed weapon
till truth outed her hypocrisy.
Bill wondered what else she had up her sleeve.

[The Rumored Boss]

A long-barreled, side-by-side Scott & Son,
it had traveled far with him
from shoots in Cuba to hunts near Venice,
safaris in Africa's greenest hills.
It ran him round £35
and stored potential mayhem in his hands.

It made a handsome picture photographed
at Club de Cazadores,
the snow-capped peak of Kilimanjaro,
or aimed in thief-plagued Finca Vigía
by a shirtless, booze-frayed Hem
whose mark left blood on the terrace outside.

Mary gave it to a Ketchum welder
who, with acetylene torch,
honored her wish, razed the Monte Carlo,
smashed the stock, and buried it in a field—
all but a scrap of lockplate
and broken bits he'd save in a matchbox.

[A Barbarian Explains Himself]

"I intend to be among the outlaws."
The road to the Abbey way
was fraught with three concerns: sheer lack of faith
in government; the rites of freedom;
and protecting the wild
from fools, states, and teeming populations.

The trio would get him labeled "racist"
in the *Utne Reader*—yes,
he opposed illegal immigration,
(*mas* toxin for an already poisoned,
overtaxed environment),
but fought the bad press till the day he died.

Son of a Postlewaite & Paul Revere,
handgun-toting classical
liberal, once used his favorite Winchester
to kill what he most despised: a TV.
Nearing death, he requested
gunfire, bagpipes, a cheerful & raucous wake.

[Billy in the Box]

Giorno and the others load the coffin:
fedora, jacket & tie,
a sword-cane of hickory, one gold coin—
a $5 Indian Head for luck
(enough to get by beyond)—
a joint of good grass and a bag of junk.

Dressed up for his trip to the underworld
in his black performing shoes,
Moroccan vest of brocade and velvet,
red bandana snug in his hip pocket,
Commandeur des Arts et Lettres
rosette in his boutonnière, and a pen.

He was near the picture of readiness
but lacking one addition.
Before the lid is closed, they slip it in:
his prized five-shot .38, "The Snubby."
John says, "This is important!
Bill believed one should always be well armed."

[He Carries the Fire]

He & Edward plotted in secrecy
to reintroduce the wolf—
the Mexican Grey—into the ur-range
of the Great Southwest; stirred by anarchy
and hatred of authoritarians.
He wisely grants infrequent interviews.

They'd say he bombed on *Oprah*, kissed Pratt's ass;
or dredge up yellowed photos:
the proto-writer dressed as a cowboy,
evil six-gun in his little southpaw.
They'd spout venom; say his ex
kept a pistol in her pussy, don't you know.

Relentlessly, he carries the fire; stokes
tinder in the cattle horn
when the words won't come and makes language burn
the binding down—no need for magical
realism, only the careful aim
of the poet who knows to squeeze and never pull.

St. Louis Gothic

A crucifix hung there above the crib
in case of extreme unction,
its empty pockets hid by Christ impaled.
No candlestick nor chrism snug inside.
Wren song in the juniper,
a nest beside the window rimmed with frost.

Brown as the Mississippi, she would come
each Wednesday for the laundry,
a cobblestone and razor in her purse.
Daddy's rich and your Mama's good-lookin'
house still as a tomb until
Lee began to voice her ironing tune.

Bottom-land-black and blue as a twelve-gauge,
thrilled & frightened all at once.
The sound glissandoed in bottleneck slides
near the crossroads of some ancient exchange.
I'd lie still, wait for Mommy,
the scent of winter in her kiss and hair.

Once with a jack-knife, quicker than pain, Lee
killed a snake in the coal bin.
Once with a whisper, gentle as rain, she'd
cursed an old possum that butchered a dove
guarding its brood in the cedar.
Once diabetes had taken her leg,

she no longer would hum when she ironed.
Once, I can't remember what
I saw, but do remember telling her
that Satan lurked outside my window pane.
I was three years old, and Lee
had put her hand across her mouth and cried.

Later, when my mother had arrived and
Lee had taken her aside,

and in a whisper hard as rain had said
Joey saw the Devil in the bushes,
Mama, worried, asked her *Lee,*
what was it, Lee? A big black dog, perhaps?

And when Lee answered, the whole world answered:
I don't know; I didn't look.
High winds made kindling of the plums that year;
the oak in the field went screaming in sleet;
I couldn't not look, so did;
I could either listen or lie, so heard.

Sestina: Querencia

The word you taught me was *Querencia*.
Its sense you revealed before it entered
the world, finding its space through your speaking
in new arenas of the uncanny.
Suggesting a shape for the familiar,
it named what's there already, though undefined.

Yet, the space of peace in chaos *is* defined
as the blood ring rages: *Querencia*.
The bull, addressing the unfamiliar,
paws runes in the dust of the realms he's entered
and by these makes sense of both worlds; a canny
surrender, wise to mutiny's speaking.

And all the while the silence is speaking,
quietly cutting through bedlam to find
a place of one's own, a home uncanny,
there in the very sound—*Querencia*.
Peace, from the heart, through the head has entered
to make one's home in the unfamiliar.

While sacred, you are no familiar
to the celebrant matador speaking
his language of disruption. He's entered
his altered state of being quite refined,
but it's the magus bull's *Querencia*
that brings down the house and rings uncanny.

A lair, a haunt, a simple space—uncanny
the way the heart can make familiar
what is never truly known. *Querencia*
whispering through the universe, speaking
through the agency of the undefined,
urging a return to what one seeks to have entered.

I knew you before your life's breath entered,
before we ever met as creatures canny

to the wind. Before you shaped or defined
my lungs, or we breathed in the new familiar,
we touched through one woman who began our
speaking—
no need for stock translations here: *Querencia*.

Once entered, even clearings unfamiliar
are named in the uncanny fires of speaking.
So now I find
        this word you taught me
                and simply write
                    Querencia.

                      —for my Father

To the Dryad in Her Eightieth Year

That story I relish has come again,
of how you instructed your first-born son,
struggling to imagine, crayon in hand,
some tree inside the garden of his head.

Distraught by his fretting, your fingers lithe,
you took the instrument and banished doubt,
drew a tree from your own accomplished well,
and in that instant, robbed him of invention.

I'll never know what tree he might have drawn,
you've fretted now for nearly sixty years.

Subsequent children you've allowed to grow
wild, nearly insolent toward creation,
their ardent frescoes riotous displays—

But what fantastic forests we have dreamed.

—for my Mother

In Nomine Something

Traces of bog under crescent moons of nails,
kohled keepsake of a day spent with kin
turning turf to the lukewarm wrath of the Dingle sun.

One knuckle swollen smooth of wrinkles,
bloodied by the crossing hitch of a *currach*'s oars
that cut through the beryl pitch of Brandon Bay.

Study these in places more haunt than home of pardon,
some means of deliverance from the covet of other lives:
on a plane, in a taxi, in the jetlag of an airport bar.

More recently at dawn in the ambush dump next door
where fifty years of rubbish lies all bust and obsolete,
like accidental faces in the lay of yellowed photos.

Read sunrise there at break of summer solstice,
let the edge of a rusted *Maytag* serve as a gnomon
then place an upright stone where it cuts the far horizon.

Reproach for such romantic bullshit follows,
excuses for the blood of origin made and shed once
more as the pendulum swings sidereal to and fro,

the need for marking where one's been or will be
in the rattletrap ride of the riddle wrought as real
far outweighing any sense of shame.

On leaving rungs of the double helix from Cork
to Connemara, waste and whiskers, collars
of saffron-umber in scores of sinks & piss troughs—

one's truest statements cling near the *Armitage Shanks*;
or twine perhaps in sheets of Belfast linen,
the orchard squandered for the sake of come again—

one thinks of how one made a gift of words
to the *col ceathar* who had a yen for writing,
then met some part of I who had come another way:

through darkness undaunted, dead in the face of the sun
to watch her break the binding, and listen to her say
Prayers, she culls from whispers, *a book of prayers.*

—*for Máire Lyne*

Nine Twenty-Four Times Nine:
A Clutch of Birthday Poems

—for Mary Cat

[Il Faut Aller Voir]

I remember the sea and the salt on my lips,
Odysseus in my head & biceps,
and you, my Penelope, patient on a beach towel;

Calypso, too, confederate with twilight,
Arranging diversions on a boat
from St. Tropez,
her argent kisses hidden
by the hand you curled against your smile.

Ocean and horizon, the almost nothing
in between: archetypal triptych
for our couched *ménage a trois.*

I held you at the Citadel,
still wish you'd bought the hat
you wore so well,
remember our nakedness
and the breeze beneath umbrella pines,

found a sign
in the stone relief:
the saint who lost his head

for love,
patron only of his own
fortuitous landfall's end,

and places
he now occupies—
tripartite, their soliloquies.

But for headless saints and *grands chapeaux*
this world is sadly lacking.

And if not for you, my love, chameleon I
would find no joy in changing.

But of missing heads and changing hats
and of saints with many lovers:
I'm out of one, one's off to you,
and I fly the other's colors.

[Geronimo]

September was Comanche subtle
that year around your birthday.

A cinquefoil's petal's worth of mornings
leading to the feast of San Geronimo
came chandeliered with lightning.

Creeks leapt shouting from their beds,
splashed chaos through the crossroads,
ignored the flashing reds
of signals pitching in the cessant calm.

Many, much, and more went missing,
left hawsers frayed
to the memory of their moorings.

The faithful found,
their beads and nails clicking,
sang missives to St. Anthony
demanding some relief.

I cited love:
quotation marks around your heart.

We, heaving gently in our rented bower,
your ribcage nuzzling my regard,
took heed of holding on.

And for a moment all was lost:

cumulonimbi beating threats
atop their penthouse anvils;
the narrowing horizon
thundering loud as heavy horses;
cyclones grinding boughs
to mere nostalgia;
my fix on the world
with all its grim unworldliness;
and any memory that
we'd ever traveled separate ways.

San Antonio rose before us
fired by a crimson fever.
But there was never any reason for alarm.
And the cause was never lost
for you and me.

[A Disambiguation in the Garden]

There is wind that shakes the olive trees
begetting interplay:

silver bellies, topsides green—

olive drab then silver
screen the petioles from constant view.

I witness this and locate you,

and me,

and what appears to be ourselves,
though done in altered hues:

two colors blurred to verdigris:
                              thaumatrope:
                                    soliloquy.

[September Moon]

Be pleased the sheets preserve
the outlines of your figure;
at night while I lie dreaming
they rustle with your name.

Be glad the earth beneath
your moving keeps impressions,
and if I lose your shadow
the dust will paint the way.

Content, my love, please be
content among your roses—
love's blush like theirs is scented,
their fragrance learned from you.

Delight, delight, my sea;
your name is my blue ocean—
you swell, I swim inside you;
I leap but never leave.

Enjoy September's moon,
its light your mere reflection;
your birth, its only meaning;
its orbit taught me well.

Beloved, be mine because
your presence is my pleasure,
confine me with your gravity—
I lap and never leave.

[Anagram: "Sonnet 18"]

Abide with me for this a moment:
I'll gather every rose you've hid or handled,
make of hours spent beside you centuries
to harm the sun's best merciless crusade.

My Cat and cool Penelope, you that are my home,
though highways rant in lethal directions,
brash sea lanes motion north,
and the low door conspires with its hinges,
still dulcet hexes steer me to your arms.

Signora, siete la mia sede 'd il mio cuore—
hasn't fever let me find dominion
and harvest a song of love?

Now send me to bed,
flesh aflame no shameful moment hath engaged.
Moths to flame are nearest to a heart song:
unto all hands rain ghosts of stars.

[Choice Un-chosen]

Life is everything we do not choose;
it occurs in spite of our best-made plans.

It falls out of our pockets,
comes all undone,
refuses to be clocked, mocked,
locked up, boxed, and outfoxed.

It taps on our windows late at night,
and will never, not ever, sweep up.

Those and them and that which we choose
are the emissaries of control.

Control itself is but deft illusion,
entertainment, no doubt,
for the whimsies of life.

That said,
I choose you—

over and over and over again—

and in so doing,
am left with contradiction:

for you
are life
to me.

As certain as
each future breath
that comes from who knows where
un-chosen, unplanned, undoubtedly under
the force of the simply is,

you are my life in every way.
I choose you and am done.

[Queen of the Fisher Kings]

I have seen her
                stand at the usual
Places: the hearth
                & the circle of stones;
Have watched her
                hands like bright anemones
Drop anchors in
                the vast ephemeral
Sea: her manifold
                beautiful guises.

I have slept with her
                in sheets of pleasure,
Have wrapped myself
                in all her graces,
& hoarded all her
                secrets to be sure.

I am rapturous in her holy weir,
  Envious & more of all she touches,
          Priapic when she weaves her gentle spell.

She mystifies man-children in her care,
  Signifies what every other couches,
          And ultimately relishes her rule.

[The Dig]

I've excavated words in the dust of diction
to see what other tongues had prepared for the smitten,
and found few that could hold love's dimensions.

Between the priest's damaging secularism
& the DJ's trip into rank mysticism,
I will seek my peace in a language yet unwritten.

Now around you indicative flashes swim
inciting my flickering tongue to form
unspeakable words concealed by your lips.

All the inhibitive articles we have stripped
from ourselves make wholly naked conversation.
They lie without power now—failures of translation.

We showed each other alphabets no one could solve;
each produced Rosetta Stones from a tangling of love.

[Remember Me]

My certainty among uncertainties,
and allow me to

rededicate myself to you,
re-manifest my love for you,
re-consecrate my soul to you

who have no un-mercies,
in spite of what the dull have said.

They, in their un-wisdom, have mistaken

passion for impatience,
justice for oppression,
vehemence for a lustful vengeance
reckless as the sea.

These who do not know you
can be forgiven and dismissed.

As for myself, there can be no such dismissal.

For I have known you all along
and I, too, in my desire
to better serve you, have mistaken

strength for cruelty,
acceptance for indifference,
righteousness for haughty pride
as crippling as disease.

Somewhere, somehow,
the woven thorns of the cynic
were pried about the head of the skeptic
as I applauded in my newfound, ill-fitting robes.

But you did not,
and carried me home
in a leavening embrace of peace.

Avatar of the enduring fire,
forgive me my many faults as a simpleton.

Think of me only as a man
who would be everything to you
who failed to understand that he already was.

Repetitio Est Filiam Oblitus Libro:

Selected Poems

FOR THEM WHAT BLINKED

Epistolary Suite:
Three Letters for Friends Gone Missing

[Thou Philip, Theif of Loco-Focos]

Hwæt! Druid of the xeriscapes, I write
To let you know that love moves
Yet in my care; fulfills your prophecy.
She rakes her thumbnails through the *caliche*
Of my heart and make roses
Go BOOM! in the dust when no sunlight breaks.

Know that your presence hangs wild in the hall;
And still the ovoid globe we
Purchased, in spite of your protestations,
Remains to date often contemplated
But uncracked and virginal:
four perspectives in a problem of paint.

I lost but one bonsai to the weather,
And all have entered autumn
Save for the myrtle. Her small death lingers
On the porch, blessed by Hecate perhaps,
Perhaps disoriented
By the northern kenning of the seasons.

We are closer now to Cahokia,
And the serpent mound rises
South and east and through a stand of poplars—
E is yet for *Eadha*, shield-maker's tree.
And well you know, Horse-Lover,
Gitchee-Gumee is not far to the north.

Last night it harried us with snow, lest we
Grow complacent and forget
The solstice comes here frozen as Dante's
Third Circle—*Wherefore art thou Longfellow?*

Does Mark Garrison still read
The *Inferno* to you in Italian?

Is he still your live model for Virgil?
You once told me (and grinned) that
His grandfather was James Whitcomb Riley,
The Hoosier poet. It reeks of him here
Along the river bottoms
And in haymows along route thirty-three.

But all in all it's not at all that bad.
The house we rent is bigger
Than the house on Duval Street.
There are maple trees that turn red and gold,
And moss grows thick on thick trunks.
That said, hearken to the disparities:

Our Green Man now hangs over the galley
kitchen doorway. Ishmael
Crouches, gilded, in our china cupboard,
And Friday's are not the same without you.
I miss our conversations,
You, chain-smoking *American Spirits*,

While exhaling transubstantiation
And Ed Dorn in the same breath—
(Sacred for Jones because it was man-made,
Profane for Olson because it had staled).
Maximus spoke with your tongue:
the thing you're after lies around the bend.

You asked me not to come back doddering—
A middle-aged professor.
What was it McMurtry wrote about friends?
…Oh yes: "*uva uvam varia fit.*"
(The grape can only truly
Become a grape by hanging with the bunch.)

So I've fallen from our vine, the wild bunch.
Yet I remain true to form.

Remember, you yourself fell from the vine
And started a new bunch in New England.
I may yet send forth green shoots
For errant currants make excellent mead.

I remain intoxicated by love.
I have not cut my long hair.
I sing when Phoebus fires my vocal rage.
I think often, fondly, of Duval Street.
I try to be more like you,
While you keep trying to be more like me.

[Anderson, The Snow Flies]

Hey, Prague on a Saturday afternoon,
remember? After having
driven six hours from post-wall East Berlin
through farmscapes ravaged by the Soviets,
there wasn't much we wanted
other than a beer, a meal, and a nap.

Remember what a son of a bitch Ed
had been that morning we left?
I was the only one in our circle
who could drive a stick & wasn't bothered
by the prospect of speeding
through Bohemia to keep up with him.

He'd gathered all the drivers together;
said he'd leave us in his dust
if we didn't haul ass Autobahn style.
When he learned I'd be driving our V-dub,
he'd rolled his eyes and snorted,
preening in his touring cap and kid gloves.

We looked at each other grinning; I laughed:
Are you going to wear that?

The look on his face was priceless, nicht wahr?
On the road we got behind him honking.
I thought he was gonna shit.
When we pulled into Prague, he shook my hand,

then screamed at Hicks for wearing that fur hat
with the hammer & sickle.
Take it off! That's no joke to these people!
When I told him Václav Havel had one
he looked at me & said Who?
Irony is lost on the mirthless.

Thought he knew everything about Prague (right).
Only came along to pose:
Bogart of the Jewish cemeteries
scribbling notes for *Rolling Stone*—what a joke.
HAND OF GLORY ROCKS EUROPE—
Lost his briefcase in a porno arcade.

You & I talked of Kafka while drinking
pilsner, buzzed in the shadow
of the castle. What metamorphoses
would we undergo in the next twelve hours?
Deterritorialized
on a regular, unnerving basis.

You told me about a photo you'd seen:
Kafka's punk-rock "granddaughter"
in black stiletto heels stomping roaches
in someplace like the men's room of Raoul's.
Singled out for misfortune,
the children of frontiersmen thus proceed.

Strange scenarios in those hinterlands:
I once saw Betty Duke's kid
in a moshpit with Lee Harvey's daughter.
Consipirators thrashing in 12/8 time—
offspring of intensity.
Killers and radicals ply the gene pool.

No such offerings at our theater
or gallery—which was it?
They listened well, applauded politely,
but never got up to dance or raise hell.
Sure, it was an early show—
Ed told us Prague shut down at 11.

Wishful thinking. Shut down himself and left
for his room with a sheaf of
stained papers under his flabby biceps
stopping long enough to tell us we had
better get some shut-eye boys,
the caravan to Berlin leaves at 10.

But we shared a bottle of cognac with
some Czech kid & his girlfriend
who told us about an after-hours club
called *Stalin* in a burned-out pedestal
that once upheld a stone Joe
himself leading hammer-toting henchmen.

Seems Mr. Havel & company blew
that eyesore to Leningrad
just before the Russian tanks iced Prague Spring.
And Jesus, what a dreamscape piled inside:
Stalin's head a chiseled skull,
the band onstage like Weil meets Iggy Pop.

Nothing nailed down: after-hours =
illegal (movable feast).
Somebody was passing round Turkish smokes,
Tobacco rolled with Moroccan hashish.
Original *Budweiser*
defied the curfew and world trademark laws.

Inevitably, we were asked to play.
Someone draped a Texas flag
(virtual twin of the starred Czech banner)
across my shoulders and we took the stage

in drunken veronicas,
the charging bull of ennui kept at bay

another night. Hordes of the converted
swelled in an upsurge of sound;
stampeding the dancefloor & barricades
of flesh, the front-stage hedonists butted
heads with the catatonic:
psycho mimes blinded in a starring match.

I swear I saw Tiresias lurking.
Snakes coupled in the cables
about the thrashing feet of stagedivers,
and I held to the mic stand unaware
of nothing but my singing
which rose, you tell me, like a vibrant scream.

A scream on loan from Theresienstadt,
no doubt. When we crossed the bridge
that spanned the dry moat surrounding its dead
silence, the hair on my neck & arms rose.
My throat tightened, my eyes burned—
against what? At the time I couldn't say.

Just another red-brick institution
for all we knew, innocent
enough until we saw the rusty gates.
Illimitable, the talent that passed
through them, and immutable
the criminal conclusions of decay.

The little two-lane highway winding through
suddenly sacrilegious.
Across the narrow straits from the death camp
a soot-stained cathedral lurched in its frame.
Saint George mumbled in his niche
too late to slay any dragons, I think.

Mock on Charybdis, your bones are numbered.
How many fled to your jaws
and away from Scylla to buy more time
with the currency of artistic pride?
You promised them protection,
and delivered nothing but moist ashes.

Massive industrial-strength fans blew smoke
from a thousand cigarettes:
bleak offerings swirling gray & pungent
in that cave of winds, tormenting the horde.
My lashes worked overtime
till the motes teared out, the beams were melted.

An ocean welled in my ears, its roaring
hounding me till I collapsed
over monitors and into the crowd
somewhere between Aeolus & Birdland
with lights throbbing in my eyes.
Revelers caught me and propped me upright

against you: we rode the verve together—
I came to lying atop
the Marshall stacks near a stone ogre's fist
still wrapped in the lone star, metamorphosed.
La cucaracha indeed.
You brought me your jacket for a pillow.

We caught a cab back down to the city.
Soldiers drank from their helmets
outside the brewery and sang, their sidearms
forged into tentative ploughshares that night.
Dionysiac cease-fire.
Didn't stick around to greet the *maenads*.

Borek & Stepanka fed us canned meat,
insisting we stay with them
playing cards and drinking Yugoslav wine
while Ed dreamt of the Autobahn & fame.

We'd hid what money we'd made
for Borek to find and curse us when we'd gone.

We hit the flea markets in the morning,
and found them holding nothing
we couldn't find cheaper in Mexico.
Posters touted jobs to Americans
wanted to teach ESL
to the nascent Boho capitalists.

Theresianstadt no longer menaced
as we sped back towards Berlin.
We spoke of dreams as we crossed its dry moats
and held the image of Christ in Dresden's
fire at bay till it burned us.
Ed didn't believe anything we'd done.

Do you suppose it was pride that spurred us?
Do you suppose we'd bartered
songs for the thrill of living utterly
freeboot for a few unsupervised years?
Think this dream will last a while?
Next time it snows in Austin we'll end it.

It's been like Thule ever since, they say.
A girl you slept with named your
child after me. I guess she like the name.
It seems now every crack UT English
grad goes teaching ESL
in Prague these days—Anderson, the snow flies.

—for Bill Anderson

[On the State of Disunion, Inter Alia]

I felt like Dylan Thomas with his hands
in the carol-singing snow,
pulling Mrs. Prothero & the fire
out the other day when I went fishing
through my stone/bone collection
and found a nugget of raw, molten lead

Paul Foreman kicked up on one of his strolls
& slipped to me one New Year's
for luck—*May this guard against broken dreams.*
I held it in my hand & remembered
how we sat on Mount Bonnel,
facing the Colorado far below.

It was St. Stephen's Day, and the Wren Song
was certainly being sung
by the neo-pagans in Zilker Park
as they gathered round the lone rock island
near the quiet football fields
brandishing their wild clubs against the birds.

Remember that night at said rock island
when you & Mary & I
saw them wreck *A Midsummer Night's Dream?*
We all agreed that Bottom was the best.
That was the first time I knew
(or at least suspected) we shared spirits.

Since then, it's been rings & harps & six-packs.
We've brewed both dark beer & mead
in your kitchen sink, and chiseled maple
into forepillars for unfinished harps—
(at least mine isn't finished)—
but let's not talk about things unfinished.

They're digging for gold on Devil's Backbone.
Enchanted Rock, Comanche

Cathedral, its pink granite dome rising
above the likes of the Nimitz Hotel,
hexed again by grave danger—
much worse than "The Harmonic Convergence."

And this time it won't just be new-agers
beating up the prickly pear
and pissing in the caverns in the name
of Gaia or other such fulsomeness,
but a concerted effort
to unhinge the spine of the Hill Country.

Not only that, but before long, Central
Texas will be a wasteland
full of Californians & neuroses—
they've been lining up in Los Angeles
since 1987:
they head east to find the "authentic" WEST,

& slash a path away from empire's end.
I heard Streisand soured a ranch
in Fredericksburg, and Brad Pitt is building
a million-dollar dump on Lake Travis
so he can swim in the raw
or drown in a "way of life" on sixth street.

What are guys like Philip going to do
when all the bookshops are closed,
and the old stone homes in the neighborhood
are all owned by lawyers & their cronies?
Nothing on the porches now
but ruin—not even wasps will nest there.

And Russell, what about spirit of place?
Who will answer when we call
from groves of hippocastus near the creek?
Were we so arrogant as to believe
that this broad & holy tump
was ours to woo with white mythology?

We should have gone camping in Terlingua
when we had the chance to go.
Or did we ever really have the chance?
We might have drunk San Pedro tea at dusk,
and tried to keep from drowning
in the quicksand in Santa Elena.

We should have talked more about the shark's tooth
I found down in Waller Creek
when I went looking for an arrowhead,
and more about the arrowhead I found
on the same small sandbar when
I looked for a second shark's tooth for you.

We should have spoken of disappointment,
of the fucked situation
you had to put up with for all those years.
But then again, I suppose the way we
handled it was the best way:
Just let the dead leaves fall when it was time.

You need to make a new ring for yourself.
To celebrate your freedom.
I wonder, did the sapphire discolor?
The green gold fade, or the red turn to rust?
Probably not. I know how
those medieval fancies never pan out.

Our golden dragons are still doing fine:
The stones are still clear & bright.
The braids are tightly woven and show no
signs of unwinding themselves from the gems.
We credit you with a great
deal of our happiness, and wish you well.

In this, your current state of disunion,
know that we still share spirits.
The fault lines shift, and lovers rise & go—
rivers rise too, and vomit elegies

in the wake that never rests;
but all of this will pass you like the sun.

Anyway, when spring comes to Wimberley
and the convolvulus blooms,
and your house & dreams are all in order,
light up a Spirit and blow the gray smoke
out across Balcones Fault—
we'll wake that bastard up when I come home.

—for Russell Strawnsmith

Letters to Woodhenge

[Why the Earth Shakes]

A good friend of mine believes
the pre-Columbian gods
have broken their ranks of slumber
to bind again with rattlesnakes
the backbone of our continent.

They have removed the sainted masks
assigned to them by conquest,
dusted off obsidian blades,
and painted their priested clowns
for war with buffalo-tail brushes.

He claims they've set Wyoming's
medicine wheels in motion,
de-christened Cahokia
as the Mississippi bleeds, then
uprooted Mound City beneath the Woodhenge sky.

The Piasa Bird circles
over Illinois bean fields,
and Quetzalcoatl
introduces himself
to border patrolmen with a switchblade and a smile.

The pale boulder which powdered
wild bones to grist for white bread
while Coyote's powers slept
is rolling to an end, he says.
In his eyes, the wild children play on quiet stones.

[Introit]

When the magalonyx & mastodon, the bones of which are now dug up, were still extant in this land of bluffs & prairies, there existed, it is said, a bird of such dimensions that it could, in its talons, easily carry off a full-grown deer or swallow whole—hoofs, hide, and horns—an antelope or buffalo. Having obtained a taste of human flesh, from that time on it would prey on nothing else. Artful as it was powerful, it would dart without warning upon a man, woman, or child and bear such off into one of the caves it haunted hewn & rugged in the bluff above the river, where it would devour the misfortunate soul. Hundreds of warriors tried for years to detroy it, but all were unsuccessful. Whole villages were nearly wiped out, and consternation spread throughout all the tribes of the Illini.

[Notes & Conversations]

How do you account for so much music
churning through the backwash, spinning out
of Wentzville, mated in the barrelhouses
to the ghosts of Gas Light Square? Jazz breakfasts
supped in dives where Joplin slept; showboats rock

in the wake towards Memphis; Mississippi
& Missouri merge like lovers near the bluffs—

Is that a reason or development?

Well, there is Cahokia: flat-topped, weird,
Shakespeherian in proportion, vast
planetarium, ceremonial magnet.

I once put my ear to its side & heard
the grass grow. It sang from ribcages
to a pulsing thrum like massive, beating wings.

[Backtracking]

In 1673, Jacques Marquette
claimed that he saw, with Louis Joliet,
a painting of what was probably two
"Water Monsters" on the bluffs near the Sioux
river portage near present-day Alton.

By 1700, these pictographic
serpents were gone. In 1936,
a novelist, John Russell, described an
image cut into the bluff: a dragon-
like creature with wings & horns: /*Pye*-uh-saw/,
"The Bird that Devours Men," (R's journal),

The site? Dynamited, quarried for stone.
Next bluff down from the blast site's gaping maw,
a State-placed plaque commemorates the meal.

[Kyrie]

*Cahokia had been a place of wealth, and did, when under the English
government, command an Extensive Indian Trade. It is not the case now.
Since the Americans have held the Country it has been Shamefully Neglected,
and many of the best families have cross.d the Mississippi, and with them
the Indian trade… there is not a building in the place that can be call.d
Elegant. There may be about 200 houses in all, but not more than half of
them Inhabited. There is little or no trade and the people are poor.*

[MOSES AUSTIN, 1783]

[Aus-Tex Proceeds from Cahokia]

When Moses Austin rode from the east
To the Mounds of Upper New Spain
In search of fortune in the silver & lead mine

Arêtes near Ste. Genevieve, west
Of the river on the Ozark Plateau,
He camped on the east bank of the Mississippi.
Since Anglo-Saxon anythings were unhappy
Visitors in *San Luis*. He & his small retinue
Washed in a pristine slough, and dressed
For prospect in silk to gain the *Alcaldé's*
Attention. With bright plumes in slouch hats,
They gamboled on horse-back till the last
Man had crossed by summons to his dais.

Empire seeded, they drifted in Piasa's reeds.

[Joplin]

It was Stark who'd postponed the syphilis
& coaxed from Washington Ave.'s brothels
a syncopation hatched in Texarkana's

cotton fields, lending it Teutonic gills
that it might breathe in heady Victorian
parlor dust & live. Now Joplin would fish

dark magic from the river to punish
Stark's pristine marches: Hanoverian,
even thin-lipped to Joplin's ears but in his hands,
twisted as any Melungeon bloodline.

So 100 years after Jefferson
bought Louisiana & all it mounds,
West-End matrons would greet 1 slave's son's vision
w/ pink lace parasols tapping in wild unison.

[Gloria]

*At length, Ouatoga, chief of the Kaokia, whose fame as a warrior reached
even beyond the great lakes of the north, sequestered himself from the rest of*

his tribe, fasted in solitude for the space of a moon, & prayed that his children would be safe from the Piasa. On the last night of the fast, a god appeared to Ouatoga, and in a dream directed him to "Select two times ten of your fiercest warriors, arm them each with a bow & poisoned arrow, and conceal every one of them in a place that I shall designate."

[Mythissippi Mud]

> "I have made a heap of all that I could find... I have
> lispingly put together this... about past transactions, [that this
> material] might not be trodden under foot."
> —NENNIUS, *Historia Brittonum*

Who is the god of this information?
A latter-day Pwyll Pendefig Dyfed,
He sits on his mound while *Moloch Mahhovet*
& *Tauroctonas*, both blazing w/ passion

Vie for his undivided attention—
While he fingers his beads & tears out his hair
Awaiting Rhiannon, his evening star,
To ride through his dreams in either direction.

Good God! Is that gateway the ship to Aeolus
Or wasteland, where Lilith the screech owl is *Rex*?

Piasa rumbles above w/ no answers—
Saarinen, *Väinämöinen*, what did you sell us?
Grafted to symbols, the steel rejects
The cornerstone pulled from the river.

[A Handful of Dust]

Long before Pound or Saarinen's folly,
Even ere Harvard & Vivien Haigh-Wood,
Long before Thames, Little Gidding & Shantih,
But after the fall of the Mound Builders, stood

Eliot, thrashed by the prospect of ragtime,
Well above bean fields, sorghum & rye,

Squinting, for sun to the west had undone him—
The Mike Finks & mark-twains, the frontiersman's sky.

While cobblestones rang near the river cathedral,
And Peabody Coalmen washed their black faces
In the jellyroll wake of the "Goldenrod,"

Tom had his moment w/ the Mississippi's drawl:
Alone, but for Woodhenge & the mounds like mesas,
He heard the voice in the wasted soil:
                              "Go," it said.

[Credo]

*Wild cattle, deer, elk, bears and wild turkeys abound everywhere, in all
seasons, except near the inhabited portions. It is usually necessary to go one or
two leagues to find deer, and seven or eight to find oxen. During a portion of
autumn, through the winter, and during a portion of spring, the country is
overrun with swans, bustards, geese, ducks of three kinds, wild pigeons and
teal. There are also certain birds as large as hens, which are called pheasants
in this country... I speak not of partridges or hares, because no one descends
to shoot at them.*
                              [FR. VIVIER, 1750]

[Saarinen]

> Väinämöinen, old and steadfast,
> Had not found the words he wanted…
> Then the aged Väinämöinen
> As a smith began to labour,
> And began to work with iron.
>   —from *Kalevala*

Sibelius left concise instruction:
Ars Finlandia—remote, brooding, sad.

But Jefferson's monument to expansion
demanded a wizard's touch, it was said.

& the city fathers turned to Eero—
nursed on the Straits of Bothnia but weaned
to American hucksters, who with grand,
shyster brags sought another Finn's *Sampo*:

a little breakthrough on a sinking raft.

What beat dictated steel parabolas?
Curved his cones while Sibelius glowered?
Solstitial arcs of the sun about soft

cedar grain? The wound in the maker's jazz?
A winged serpent droning from a potsherd?

[Burroughs]

Every plains tribe had its honored berdache
who served the beat by syncopating styles.
Mound City's was no different. Still, the drawls
of its heir to fortune in ticker tape slash
the western shore, cutting a swath of words
across that same frontier which vexed T.S.,
but sent wild Wm. in Quantrill's Kansas
war-wake marauding, fierce, while other bards
looked over burdened shoulders toward the dawn.

'Tain't no sin to take off your skin, & dance—

Headlong into that breach thence to Birdland,
Frisco, & the N.Y. Bunker, where the wan
Toby, shade like Virgil, spake of Lawrence,
of ribcage & wing, of whispered legend.

[Offertory]

The village is composed of Tamarois, Cahokia, some Michigans and Peorias. There are also some Missouri cabins, and shortly, there are to come about thirty-five cabins of this last named nation who are winterquartering some ten or fifteen leagues from here below the village on the river… The Tamarois and Cahokias are the only ones that really form part of this mission. The Tamarois have about thirty cabins and the Cahokias have nearly twice that number. Although the Tamarois are at present less numerous than the Cahokias, the village is still called Tamaroa, Gallicized "Des Tamarois," because the Tamarois have been the first and are still the oldest inhabitants and have first lit a fire there, to use the Indian expression.

[FATHER BERGIER, FEB. 1700]

[Swimming Near the Guardrail]

We parked on the shoulder of the hwy.
And dreamed we saw what the passing Sioux saw
Thundering once through clouds on cloisonné

Wings: the painted semblance of *Piasa*—
Feathered serpent of the Illinois tribe,
Cannibal Spirit, devourer of men—
Years before Marquette, "black buffalo robe,"
Crossed the Chain of Rocks & vexed the Mandan.

We limped along the river jetty, you
Found the bleached shell of a snapping turtle.
The bluffs were useless palisades. Below,

A south-bound grain barge disturbed these subtle
Reflections: the bluffs' retouched "pictographs"
& *Piasa* (the tugboat's name) in "glyphs."

January Thaw

Green as mistletoe in chinquapin trees
That lined the two-lane into Arkansas,
2 kids rolled through the January thaw—
For Whom the Bell Tolls rested on her knees
As she read aloud to him while he steered
The '40 Ford down old Rte. 66
To Hot Springs (off State 7) where they shared
A honeymoon kiss between motor checks.

Toltec Mounds near Little Rock, Heavener's
Rune Stone to the west, & Cahokia
North & east, formed a mystic triangle

That cradled every thought they, as lovers,
Would breathe in passion to say *Make me a
Child…* How futures begin to commingle.

[Sanctus]

*Near the place of concealment, another warrior was to stand in open view
as a victim for the Piasa, which they must shoot the instant it pounced upon
its prey. When the chief awoke next morning, he gave thanks &, returning to
his tribe, told of his dreams. The warriors were selected quickly & placed as
directed in ambush.*

[James Arthur Defenestrates Winter]

The house: brought up in pieces from the river
On flat-beds like some Gypsy carnival,
Each plank scarred with a Roman number—
Permutations of X— I— V— over
Window latches and new marks that he cut
To plot each solstice & its equinox
Since that first sun, through frost & parallax,
Told him one Saint John's: *I have not gone out!*

Across the Mississippi, old Woodhenge
Heard the same in Cahokia's' shadow.
Now light pinballs off its cedar-post flange.
X marks the spot where I snapped a photo:
Monks Mound & my father bathed in umber—
Skies like open windows in December.

[The Delta Queen in Dire Straits]

At odd times in autumn I'd sometimes ride
up the river road. Bluffs like chiseled gauze
sculpted in Pangaea's urwälder billowed
in the waning Indian summer haze.

I'd shut my eyes for seconds at a time,
ride one-handed doing 80, or stand
on the footrests like a Gypsy errand

boy—*fate* a pleasant hazard of the game.

One dusk, ferried by the Golden Eagle,
I joy-rode the sloughs of Calhoun County.

Apple-stands & pumpkins lined the uplands,
but in the bayous all was a tangle.

There I saw the big water Manitou;
its stern wheel straining in the shallow bends.

[Agnus Dei]

*The island of the Holy Family, which conceals the view of the Mississippi
from the French settlement as well as from the Indian village of the Kaokia,
measures one league or more in length by nearly one half of a league in width
and is completely covered with a forest of full grown trees good for building
purposes or for fuel, especially quantities of cottonwoods but very few walnuts
and mulberry trees. It is almost everywhere covered with rushes, which our*

horses seek greedily. When the waters of the Missouri and Mississippi rise very
high, the greater part of the island is flooded...

[FR. MERCIER, 1735]

[Brubeck Serenades the Snow Queen]

Between Monks Mound & the Mississippi,
The vast alluvial east bank's shallows
Sprawl beside mud flats held in by oxbows,
While the skyrocket flanks of Our Lady
Guard waters & snows like some mothership

Poised, waiting perhaps for Parousia's
Bugle, getting instead this euphonious jazz—
Christ & be-bop in a glorious crack-up.
His Mass: an attempt to unite the fragments,
The botched business unresolved—Masada,
The fierce, imperial Roman blood-vent—

In Brubeck, the renegade Essene, innocence
& blood ties the great western *horrida*
To this place, this haunt of the horned serpent.

[Desmond Takes Five from Dying]

When Brubeck started playing his 'Take Five'
That night long ago at *The Plantation*,
We knew it couldn't fly w/out Desmond,
But cheered in spite of the poor judgment Dave
Had made in ending the show w/ this tune.
I mean, everybody knew that cancer—
Of the lungs—
              had crippled Paul's saxophone.

This was his trademark:
                    beat, tone & measure.

Desmond's replacement, a baritone man,
Slinked off the stage like a fading mirage.

A beautiful alto, just like breathing,

Cool & slow, began to croon 'Take Five,' then
Someone was taking the stairs to the stage,

& suddenly, Desmond was there—*playing.*

[Communion]

Ouatoga offered himself as a victim, willing to die for the tribe. Placing himself in open view of the bluff, he soon saw the Piasa perched above, licking its gore-flecked maw and eyeballing him like certain prey. Ouatoga drew himself up to his utmost height and, planting his feet firmly on the earth, began to chant his holy death song. A moment later, the Piasa spread its wings; it rose in the air, and, swift as a thunderbolt, darted down upon the chief, matching his chant with ominous silence.

[Desmond & the Piasa Bird]

To sloughs where water hyacinths gathered
Life from the peaty murk of the sawyers,
Came Desmond the bold. Armed w/ a slayer's
Requisite failures, he clutched the battered
Sax in hand crying *Piasa come forth!*
The thundering wonder & lightning-bug
Twilight erupted w/ rumbles & froth
Of the long mound dead turning in the drag.

Desmond stood rapt on the Great River Road,
Twice-blessed the bluffs & the ship-wakes of tugs,
Put bog reed to lips, & uttered the charm.

The rhapsody pierced the man-eater's side—
Muse locked w/ Chronos in two dialogs;
Made brothers of flesh & of ideogram.

78

[Star-crossed]

The last time around the prospectors freaked—
Afraid the desert would melt into glass.
Some hurried burros through landscapes that cracked
In the heat, & brother Helios
Burned holes in the heads of meteorites
That showered like Perseids through the dross
& filings: ice-smelt leaving of the comet's
Wrenching glans. Others were not as remiss.

One prepared for the coming disaster—
Plucking his beard in a parched arroyo;
Nailing himself to a Joshua Tree.

A deputy sheriff, not long after,
Found him laughing in a grim falsetto
Half-ass crucified, his hammer hand free.

[Benedicamus]

Scarcely had he reached his victim, when every bow was sprung & every arrow was sent to the feather into its body. The Piasa uttered a wild, fearful scream that resounded far over the other side of the river, and expired.

[AN. I ^M. DCCCCXCVII. HER ÆTEOWDE SE FEAXEDE STEORRA]

[*1997: Here Appered the Long-Haired Star*]

We went to bear witness:
    the long-haired star
Parading its standard
    over powerhouse
Of glittering skyline
    & carapace

Of progress soldered
                to the bones of yore,
As well as above
                the much dimmer fields
In a landscape thrashed
                by opposable thumb,
Tornadic fury,
                & hundred-year flood.
We went like water
                towards a time-ravaged dam.
Atop the Mound,
                we looked west at Easter
Waning stainless
                from the steel of the Arch,
While Woodhenge caught
                the last rays in her web.
Only the river,
                serpentine past there,
Bore witness to the kiss,
                the brushing reach
Of man & woman,
                the moon's tonsured ebb.

[FUTHARK 2K]

ᚠ

[*feoh*] Wealth

First-plucked by the old diplopic one-eye
crucified with his halo of blackbirds,
reeking of some revenant Valhalla.

It debuted hung midst the wealth of boneyards,
buzzing like St. John's Wort in the brain-pan
of a doe-eyed, suicidal co-ed.

Awaiting orders, couched in frigid stone
it puts the bite in *feudal, fuck,* and *fee,*
and spawns the savage grace of savage men.

ᚢ

[*ur*] The Wild Ox

Ur-portrait of the ferocious aurochs,
but more as well: epithet of trouble
moving towards man-meat through the barley stalks.

Eat or be eaten thou execrable.
Here reside the first-strike & force or arms.
Here lie both Waco & Zimbabwe's rubble.

Contrapasto stance of the one who maims
first & questions later: be he Podunk
sheriff, punk or president, his way's harm's.

ᚦ

[*thorn*] The Thorn

Thanatos & persistent memory
kept it stabbing well into the Xian
era, though misread by moderns as Y.

It's said it's the thorn that pricks everyone.
It's a torn blouse too, and a tricycle
no one rides; a size 7 barbed-wire crown.

None but Thalia can feed it now, fickle
dragon preening atop the hoard of time.
It's the lisp in "scythe" & sweep of the sickle.

ᛝ

[*ansuz*] Language

Answers. Signals. Answers. The source of words.
One man's speech is another man's sentence.
Best be like Sigurd and talk to the birds.

The language of the sky's an eloquence
few men can understand. More's the pity
language, more than music, can raise offense.

One tongue to brandish death or clemency.
The unsaid thought spinning past fruition:
wisdom's deferment; breach of prophecy.

ᚱ

[*rad*] Riding

Roads converging in vast desert reaches ·
(have no doubt riding is worse for the horse)
bear signs of the suffering of creatures.

Dark flesh caught in spines of the prickly pear
confirms ~~rumors of~~ [sic] *local slave trade route.*
It's all there jack in sun-baked semaphore.

Wile miles remembering, must not forget.
Tell who drove whom round the "forgetting tree"—
who taught the yahoos how to mount & ride.

⟨

[*cen*] The Torch

Κύριε ἐλέησον, Χριστέ—No.
This was supposed to be the living flame,
the keen edge of light conquering shadow.

Instead, the keen of loss shakes the Kingdom.
The Lord's barge is lit and pushed out to sea.
Two words scratched in the sand—VERE DIGNUM—

are swept aside by the tide's unmercy.
The torch is now perverted as it burns
2x4s cruciform against the sky.

ᛉ

[*gyfu*] The Gift

Give way. The sign says YIELD at the crossing:
confused intersection of need & want
where greed and gain are most prepossessing.

Paganini. Robert Johnson. Both went
seeking fame at the crossroads—made the scene—
but neither thought to ask how much he'd spent.

Gaining or losing, there's no in-between
when on fire we wake in collective thirst,
reach for water, and guzzle gasoline.

ᚹ

[*wyn*] Joy

Won. I won. Mine is joy and salvation.
His desiccated crosier greens with blooms,
though none fairer than those in which I've lain

nursed by the *Hörselberg,* mountain of dreams,
wiled by her *Heldenbrüst* too. The forest
rings, for here the peregrine *Ritter* comes.

83

Curse not the winter crooknecks as Venus
woos among them when the passion vine croaks.
And I shall never keep her from her lusts.

ᚺ

[*hægl*] Hail

Hail of bullets. And a plague of 'public servants'
spreads throughout the land. The despot's artless
storm-troopers flex their blind allegiance.

One hears things like SIC SEMPER TYRANNIS.
This stone-cold bitch too's gone bad in the teeth.
Tip the scales, Astræa, with Attic grace.

Melt this coldest of kernels: civic wrath.
Mark the end of insidious misrule
from all sides so the Republic can breathe.

ᚾ

[*nyd*] Need

Need is bound fast by an odd symmetry
to giving. X spins out of Y's control,
goes cart-wheeling through the heart's poverty-

stricken ghettos where Jack the Ripper strolls
hand in hand with Harpo Marx and Jesus.
Christ, Killer, consummate fool. The heart's full

of such ludicrous inconsistencies.
One constant: the need to give drives the lot
wavering between war & consensus.

ᛁ

[*is*] Ice

Is cold & slick. Is the haunt of Loki.
Is primal matter. Is life emergent.
Is the drowned city. Is the city's sky.

The politician. The trickster's pageant.
The harsh beginning. The wolf is hunting.
The lure of Europe. The folk divergent.

[N.B.] Tribes blind to their own sins say it's the fang
that vampirized their brethren to the north,
made them take delight in cyclic killing.

ᛦ

[*ger*] The Year

Years spiral out of years and into more,
mazing through the roundabouts undeterred.
Yet at the pulsing hub, some Minotaur

switches signs and a Vauxhall clips a Ford.
Time stops—shares with space insurance info.
The bull god thunders. Scratches. He is bored.

Fierce horns like dream-catchers in the window
punch out the spokes of history again
till some Theseus in his tow truck shows.

ᛇ

[*eoh*] The Yew

You, the cradle & coffin of the vine,
we all know you're at home in the witch-grass.
So just how many tongues have fed your kin?

And were they directing Epaminondas,
swilling blood of the black bulls with Hecate,
or were they simply in the way, speechless

with fear, expendable at best, scape-goats?
If your roots do spread to every jawbone,
let's hear from those who never got to shout.

ᛈ

[*peorth*] The Game

Putsch comes to mind. In the beer hall the dice
cup clatters, and all the lucky ones laugh
as the unlucky are made to undress.

The scholars are sufficiently vexed: half
translate the lacuna thus: ["apple tree"]
while ["penis"] is picked by the other half.

So the odd game remains a mystery.
It's outcome, unfortunately, does not—
we've bones, teeth, numbers to tell the story.

ᛉ

[*eolhxsecg*] Marsh Grass

Elk brooding about the fens bore witness
to the tromping phalanx of Hadrian,
greeting with snorts & whistles its progress

through the sedge. *Gladius* slashed for years then
became 'elksword.' Later marsh-grunts bled pus
in the vernacular of Jute & Dane.

Sharp tongues must dull with time—(**gladiolus**
n [L 'sword,' **Celt** origin (*cleddyf*)] 1: Plant
w/ sword-shaped leaves, bright flowers)—they must.

ᛋ

[*sigel*] The Sun

Solarcaine's now a useless remedy.
A 'coppertone,' they warn, is as reckless
as having unsafe sex with a junkie.

What delight we took in the morning rays
we've swapped for the fear of metastasis.
So much for light and the cult of Mithras.

What dark bull has made us its devotees?
Crouched in caverns with no faith in the sun
we're burnt offerings to the CFCs.

↑

[*tir*] A Star

Take a fix on your position. From here.
From there. Which side of the proscenium
arch suits you best? Answer but don't answer.

You're walking on graves but you don't see them.
Awed by the quick flare of a shooting star,
coming apart in the pursuit of fame.

Resist the urge to change all that occurs
into entertainment, and then get packed—
Your goddamned fifteen minutes are over.

ᛒ

[*beorc*] The Birch

Beth they called you when your switches were used
in the beating of bounds and delinquents.
Charm you were from lightning, evil & wounds.

The ghost who glides with a hat of birch haunts
not the living, but returns to heaven
accepting death with utter compliance.

Now the woods are one vast birch-hat. Seven
to one birch outnumbers the other trees.
Are we leaving soon? Going, going, gone.

ᛗ

[*eh*] The Horse

Found: Hag-ridden at cock-crow in the byre,
taut in a muck-sweat, panting like bellows,
with bleeding sides & sores on its withers,

one horse beaten with a charred holly bough.
Appears to have been recently gelded.
Lost: Small mettlesome mare thirteen hands high,

cream colored, bluish of eye, & clean limbed.
CAUTION: May be a danger to children
and other horses. Small reward offered.

ᛗ

[*man*] The Human Being

[…] *no such thing as "inhuman" behavior.*
Each act that horrifies, shocks & sickens,
makes the ignorant man cringe & utter

his [STATIC] *rhetorical speech-amends*
to ward off his [GARBLED] *notions of fear,*
bears the clear mark of Homo sapiens.

So turn in your guns & welcome your brothers:
cannibal, Nazi, thrill-killer, pimp, ["Whoo!"]
butcher, breaker, snuff-film-maker [APPLAUSE].

ᛚ

[*lagu*] The Sea

ZULU TIME 0803: Off port side,
three men overboard. All engines stopped. Left
full rudder broke the five flag & lowered

to the dip. 0805: Motor whale boat
water borne proceeding to pick up men.
CONFIDENTIAL: Am now convinced without

a doubt that I have angered Poseidon.
CHANGE COURSE: 295°r (clock wise).
I will feel better when I have eaten.

◆

[*ing*] The God of Fertility

IN . GRATIA . TIBI . IN . VITRO—Sirs,
with sperm levels dismally low we laugh,
for the orchard's wracked by bombs & coat hangers.

Keep my garden to myself till it's safe
to sow my seed; too damned many people
in this world for it to feed. Wheat from chaff

'she' winnows when 'she' chooses. It's simple:
you don't. The line grows not thick but distant.
All but heretics now we raze the temple.

ᛉ

[*ethel*] Native Land

Εθνος & Εθος sheltered in its hills.
We got so close that we could see stubble
fires burning, and into light sleep I fell.

The smell of burning cedars, though it was subtle,
brought me thoughts of Neritum after rain.
I dreamt of bread & wine upon my table.

The last best thing broad on the horizon,
up in the sea towards sunset did it lay.
My home. And when I woke up it was gone.

ᛞ

[*dæg*] The Day

Dawn breaks with the song of the darkling thrush.
Where's the six-gun poet of honest means?
Gone the way of séances, absinthe & hash.

Orféo's up from the underword sans
the prize but he's got a kick-ass new style,
his own talk show, and a shitload of fans

He campaigns for womyn's rights, chews his smile,
loves when the script reads [*Lets go of her hand*].
Carpe per diem, asshole—yer paid in full.

ᚠ

[*ac*] The Oak

Achaean & Angelcynn each assert
that circling an oak cures any illness.
The worst of plagues will pass to the first bird

to lite in the twigs of the tree thus dressed.
Achaean & Angelcynn vie to score
new lands borne by sails cinched to oaken masts.

Achaean & Angelcynn storm the shores
and form a conga line round the hard wood.
Words & acorns scatter in a fever.

ᚠ

[*æsc*] The Ash

Ash-pit of history [the leitmotif]—
Enter YGGDRASIL *trailing roots & twigs,*
its ropes & rigging lashing the GOOD THIEF.

THE CHORUS: (*gravely*) Get the wheel's cogs
turning each Wednesday. Give us a creed.
Never mind, old friend, that Gog & Magog

are spoiling for a rhubarb in the woods.
Your mission, that is should you accept it,
is guard the taproot & tickle the dead.

ᚣ

[*yr*] The Bow

Yew again in the guise of τοξιχον,
a kore's grin for those about to fall.
The stranger takes it up, sees the omen

sent by Saturn, strings it with the skill
of a bard winding a peg of his lyre,
speaks when the arrow threads each handle-hole.

Only husks of words fill the doomed men's ears:
blah blah FORTUNE *yadda* RAPE *blah blah* WIFE
yadda yadda VENGEANCE *blah blah* SEVEN YEARS

ᛡ

[*iar*] A Sea Creature

I have swam [sic] *through libraries and sailed*
through oceans... I am... earnest... I will try.
There are...preliminaries to [be] *settle*[d].

Sic[k]bed is it? Suppose that's apropos.
Cuchullain did some of his best work there.
In a sense, he'd his Leviathan too.

None more troublesome than this *mal de mer*—
INGREDIENTS: One big white nightmare stalked
by a multicultural crew. Beware.

ᛗ

[*ear*] The Clay

Earlier, some things were said that—Recall
the editor's rune for *human being*,
depicted as a creature capable,

if not accepting, of dark commission.
Well, here he goes further, illustrating
a deep-seated mortal apprehension

of—well, simply put, death. BOO! Here's the thing:
molecular transubstantiation—
PLEASE STAND BY. WE ARE EXPERIENCING—

❉

[…] The Unknowable

[CHANNEL 9]: *Some things are best left unknown.*
Those who gaze with remote uncertainty
on the deeds of gods—[FLIP TO CHANNEL 10]:

Are these the shadows of things that will *be…*
[QUICK FLIP FROM 10 TO 6 THEN BACK TO 10]:
or the shades of things that may *be, only?*

[FLIP TO 8]: *—'s quite possible, I mean,*
there's just one thing that can't be avoided.
But in the end, no one cares any—[9]:

The Chord

All the miseries of mankind come
from one thing, not knowing
how to remain alone.
                    —BLAISE PASCAL

We find comfort only
in another beauty, in others'
music, in the poetry of others,
though solitude may taste like
opium…
                    —ADAM ZAGAJEWSKI

F:

Floating, falling, both and neither. Spinning webs in zero
        G. A tangle of perception and a tango of deceit.
        A crucial fix for the suffering voyeur who,
        blinded by desire, rants into the westerlies: *Ah,
        Vanitas! Your name is composition, your music my
        demise. Even lashed to the mainstay I cannot stay
        my blood. It swells towards you in vast erections…*

Fortuna whispers a malady of singing—*una canto triste*—
        implied by the opening strains. Subdominant
        to sorrow, the cellos ooze libido through salient
        f-holes as the runner stalks the gangplank. Even
        his name is an unresolved sadness: A curse in

a bottle poured forth from Penzance bleeding
westward in a full-out riptide towards an ending
just beginning, a demolition debut.

Alone, he is cocksure, cuntsure, cool, collected, poet.
He is dragonslayer, soothsayer, champion,
workaholic. With others he grows distant, and
sweet discord is his muse. His obligatory wound
bleeds a trinity of grieving: Patricide, fratricide,
the cliché cup of venom poured down his gullet
by the object of his hunger.

There is a crucible in his mind and in his future in which
a woman's hand brushes strands of fire from her
eyes. Then will they see him clearly as he sees
her. Then will a crisp new dolor be exchanged
for the old bedraggled anguish in their cache.
Till then the reckless messenger sets forth in the
key of sea resolved to OD on the absent tonic
he would snort like contraband.

B:

Bound to a catechism unvexed by philosophy, she lands
the first blow in the breaking of his will. Love
soon learns him how to hide her letters, pictures,
the lock of auburn she sends one winter's eve.
And he finds himself as Savitri—an androgyne
contemplating the cosmos in a mud hole. *O
petite mort. Mysterium tremendum.* Every lackey
come a lover is a mystic.

Behind this world is left another, beneath this wound a
star. Beyond this blade of bitter poison shines
its better brother—the edge of resurrection,
its bloodgutter wracked like the cock of Osiris

dragged from the mouth of the metafish—its damage fitting the wreck of his *doppelgänger's* skull. How passion rapes her anger as she lowers to his throat the polished cant.

Can her climb through the sea wracks towards him tip the scales of euphony? She of a kingdom in 6/8 time, who in mounting the breastworks of duty he once raised about him, dismantles obligation with a brief, dismissive wave? How steeled can either be to the stripping of such armor? And yet she climbs, small & deadly, fervor's dagger in her teeth & in her heart.

Run clean through by an unmarked redemption he submits to her for the breaking. She, rose rampant from another king's garden, crowns him worthy of her brambles. She binds his wounds & his desires; she has him by the balls & whispers: *All that is not useful shall be burnt away.* The black zodiac is circling when the pact they forge forever is blessed by the chaos moon.

G#:

Gazing at the fourteenth phase of the *The Twenty-Eight Incarnations* his majesty nearly succumbs to a belief in "The Wheel." How else to explain such perceptions? Cuckoldry haunts his sleep as the courier woos his intended. Sensing he is but one half of a ruptured whole he broods while the stone of kinetic fury, coal-black & virulent, bursts dehiscent in his belly.

Gesamtkunstwerk, his wizards tell him, sharpens the blade of being. They suggest a diversion— he malingers amusing himself by scoring arrangements in ink: colorful flesh wounds in the hides of his serfs & bondswomen, the brutality of his vision matched only by the fierce tattoo of the war drum in his head. Even savagery aspires to music. It shapes the sky with howls & panting.

Boiling with wrath & final solutions, he vows to end the fallacious trysting and is older in the morning for having done it. He blinds himself with Jesus, denies his rival's coarse sonata: *Pedicabo ego vos, O et irrumabo*. When his teeth tear through the dot of "flesh" his lady's tongue is elsewhere. By the time the smoking censer clears, his Christ is in the house of vengeance.

He muses: *We know why the prodigal return—but not for the lives of me why they are so welcome*. Twelve steps, twelve tones, and twelve bewildered friends all in need of a smug conductor, all zombie round in routine mutiny, round the spokes & coils poised, crossing & forever crossing hubs of please-god begging, arriving broke & incognito at their worn-out, predetermined site.

D#:

Debilitating absence of the governing hedge dividing self from the other: this was her love's abiding condition & bane of her own existence: *I will own that his state is a puzzle of being, one quite opposed, I will own, to my own*. Her thick, if coolly translucent partition between one & many (*do any I own?*) allows such a freedom she shall not surrender: *I own this I own & I ever will own*.

Damn every-sharp-day-here's swell toward St. John's—
a part of each waxing, a part of each wanes.
How many nights has she lain awake praying
he'd find i n herself the peace that he craves,
to only discover—filled with his fire—that only
she ever his loneliness raised. *Why must he be
hungry, so hungry for* us? *Why can't he be happily
vested in* me? *Why can't he be happy, O happy
with* me?

One breaks. One dissembles. One bleeds as he
croons. And the burden he shoulders can't
cover the wound. She watches him well with
connectedness, watches. Watches him fill to
the brim, and she watches. Watches him spill
from the sides, and still watches. He's spilling
out ailing, ailingly spills into so many others it's
easy to track him, easy to choose; choose one
from among them.

*But one who is not him won't do. There is but only one
solution and that solution is*—sui, sui, sui *side by
side;* sui *side by side by side with everything and
him.* But who should go and who remain, and
who must stay behind? *Seditious, the spring of
discordant thinking, subversive the corners swept
clean; still I hear it:* sui, sui, sui *side by side;* sui
side by side by side with everything—but me.

Thumbnails For a Portrait of Sacher-Masoch

I

DIE KUNST DES JÄGERS

Territorial pissings around the perimeter
| Possessives knifed in birch bark where
the women bleed | Females in effigy fash-
ioned from tusk & antler | One hope one
hunger for both stone & chisel | Tortured
frescoes scrawled by a dark spelunker
| Veneration of the cross ideal | Bright shib-
boleth branded in willing flesh | A tribe of
o n e | Blood-welt handprint spanked o n
the dotted line | Altars makeshift in the
snowbound copse | S i g n & symbol of
contracted submission | Trussed urgency
in the w h i p l a s h e d pleas | O merciful
unmercy | Come | A n d the moon does
not a n s w e r such dumbstruck howling |
Who beseeches the stalked o b s e s s i o n |
Who in turning stakes the claim

II

DIE KUNST DES BAUERS

Lashed to the frame is the cultivar | New
flower risen from a cleft in the order | The
hunter's dagger beaten for a plow share |
She reins in p u l l i n g taut at the bridle |
Who b i n d s the tongue | Who sings desire
| Who wraps the breast in ermine | Leash
& leader wind a b o u t a gentle fist | Who
guides his plodding | The f u r r o w s are
worked according to their w i s h e s | The

which are shared and pass between the
reins | Lashed to the frame is the cultivar
| New f l o w e r risen from a cleft in the
ardor | Astrakhan sashes n o w plaited to
thrashers | Master is mastered is slave is
e n s l a v e r | Who in turning stakes the
claim

III

DIE KUNST DES ÖLMALERS

A frail Madonna vexes the spoiled canvas
| Brushes crafted from one's own lashes |
Cedar dust black sand and nails prime the
tempera | V e n u s hairs grace the gesso |
Perhaps a severed ear t h r o u g h the mail
slot | In the end there is desperate plead-
ing for the whip | Who would break such
diabolical beauty would become its play-
thing | The redeemer puts Her foot down
| There | And the mountain where S h e
lives is littered with crusaders | Who prey
so they praise for they m u s t so they pray
| Sie ist ein Teufel | Eine Göttin | Ich liebe
sie | But the painter the r u i n the eye of
the s t o r m | Who h o l d s the mirror is
shared a n d shattered | Who in turning
stakes the claim

IV

DIE KUNST DER HEILERIN

Invitations delivered by proxy at midnight
| A threadbare Persian showing signs of
traffic | Trespassing fancy of the obedient
knee | Left here | Right there | The lash

traces a g a i n the constellation of scars |
The sky of his flesh is b r u i s e d like slow
twilight | How She strains against the bit
of Her passion | Desire is the power in His
fist again | Desire is Him and is her | Thus
the r a d i c a l nostrum | Thus the rival's
beating | Deliver us from love's unreason
and o t h e r evils | Shake surrender like
s t o l e n silver from our coats | Turn us
from obsession | Turn us f r o m ourselves
| T u r n us into you | Who in t u r n i n g
stakes the claim

Sestina for the Birds

We sit on the porch swing
and listen to the mockingbird
while April drinks the rain
just starting to fall
in long and sodden whispers
around the hedges.

Some wrens in the hedges
chirp like the chains of the porch swing
while we speak in whispers.
The spry mockingbird,
in whistles that rise and fall,
serenades the rain.

In an eavesdropping rain
of tiny blossoms, the hedges,
bustling with wrens since fall,
shake near the porch swing.
A wren scolds the mockingbird
and our dry whispers.

Giggles rise from whispers
as we weather her chilly rain
of ire. The mockingbird
buzzes the hedges,
and then lights on the porch swing
chain as blossoms fall.

Who would care should we fall
from grace in a hail of whispers
sitting on this porch swing
mocking the wren's reign
over her brooding hedges?
Would the mockingbird?

Head cocked, the mockingbird
leaves the chain. His wings rise and fall,

shrugging as he hedges
our bet with whispers.
He lights on a branch as rain
drenches the porch swing.

The porch swing is empty. The mockingbird
bathes himself in the rain. Wren feathers fall:
whispers and curses rattle the hedges.

—for Mary Cat

Unaccompanied:

Songs
FOR DISTANT MUSIC

Pontiac Flanagan

there's an old Illinois cornfield that the Piasa calls home
where a Flanagan named Pontiac lives too
in the backseat of a Cadillac where the vines overgrown
have hidden his haven from view
enough corn to feed Cairo and crow to feed Cable
enough water to keep Willow in tears
he could drink half of Champaign right under the table
talk Cicero clean up to its ears

he haunted the medians for mirrors and hubcaps
that he'd nail to a sassafras tree
and he kept his reflections in a piece of old burlap
but he never left one you could see
and the first time I saw him he stood in the mirror
I must have been just about three
it was all so obscure but it all got much clearer
that his face was where my face should be

sometimes I used his eyes or he used mine for staring
we could lie through the other one's teeth
it was not so much sharing as just being or wearing
the way a knife might sometimes wear a sheath
and the knife had a dish but the dish done got broken
when it met with a demitasse spoon
the spoon shoveled sugar till the last word was spoken
it just burst like a big red balloon

it was moonshine on Mondays on Sundays just water
and he once named me Saturday's prince
and he fed me on fodder that he'd saved for the daughter
that he'd fathered but had never seen since
and he once fell in love with a girl from St. Louis
whose mother had christened her Nell
and we went to their wedding but nobody knew us
so we just took turns ringing her bell

Rimbaud Diddley

l'absinthe buvons ce soir
je ne m'occupe plus de ça

je ne veux pas une jambe en bois
je ne m'occupe plus de ça

Rimbaud Diddley
Rimbaud Diddley
Rimbaud Diddley
Rimbaud Diddley

de la poésie ne parlez pas
je ne m'occupe plus de ça

ma jambe ne découpez pas
je ne m'occupe plus de ça

Rimbaud Diddley
Rimbaud Diddley
Rimbaud Diddley
Rimbaud Diddley

dans Charleville ne m'enterrez pas
je ne m'occupe plus de ça

l'Afrique, je me demande pourquoi?
je ne m'occupe plus de ça

Rimbaud Diddley
Rimbaud Diddley
Rimbaud Diddley
Rimbaud Diddley

Vendidi Fumar (I Sell Smoke)

vendidi fumar
I sell smoke
vendidi fumar
I sell smoke

pick it up at market
put it in your pocket
drive it but don't park it
slip it in the socket

push it through the keyhole
listen to me *mijo*
vendidi fumar
I sell smoke

vendidi fumar
I sell smoke
vendidi fumar
I sell smoke

keep it in the bottle
till you're in the saddle
open up the throttle
listen to it rattle

so good for what ails ya
until it derails ya
vendidi fumar
I sell smoke

fire! fire! it's a fire sale
fire! everything must go
buyer! buyer! it's a fire sale
buyer! here's what you don't know

vendidi fumar

wrap it round your eyeballs
laugh at all your rivals
slap it round your low balls
trap it with your bibles

float it on the high tide
blow it out your backside
vendidi fumar
I sell smoke

caveat emptor
caveat emptor
caveat emptor
I sell smoke

vendidi fumar

fire! fire! it's a fire sale
fire! everything must go
buyer! buyer! it's a fire sale
buyer! here's what you don't know

fire! fire! it's a fire sale
fire! let the buyer beware
fire! fire! it's a fire sale
buyer, it's the flames we share

vendidi fumar

Melungeon in the Dungeon

hocus pocus 6th & Locust
burnt bituminous coal
broke a lot of brickbats cross my back
but they never did touch my soul

queevy quavy English navy
stinkalum stankalum stilt
shook apart the wall when the shylock sheriff
shut me in the prison he built

step around the corner in a coal-black shadow
and a jacket bought with last month's rent
cobble in the pocket when I sank it like a rocket
with the hounds pickin' up my scent

spoke Melungeon down in the dungeon
Mississippi river boat came
standin' on the levee with the cotton gettin' heavy
in the Hannibal, MO rain

mixed my magic in the median muddy
where the blacktop blackguard don't go
sic 'em in the sycamore, big chief Sagamore
wampum blacker than crow

took a little solace from a looker down in Hollis
who was tetchy as an Ozark witch
fixed dumb supper just before she let me tup her
but I woke up in a roadside ditch

you'd not a-wanna been me had you seen me
haulin' down the Osage trace
had a little drink o' gin, skull up in a chinquapin
helped me ratchet up my pace

possum up a sweet gum, raccoon shotgun
shoutin' on the shoulder at dawn
fish Tenkiller with a wishbone trot line
trace my tracks they's gone

just in case the Choctaw Nation
didn't want me passin' through
paint my body like a buffalo berdache
stick a feather in my shoe

rest my bones in betwixt of the four-lane
stumbled on a pitch-roofed crypt
tibiae, fibulae, scapulae, jawbone
homespun britches done ripped

slept all day in the dust of a suicide
Oklahoma called her bluff
somebody grievin' her down in Heavener
must have left the rune stone stuff

crossed Red River on a barque I made of junipers
and paddled to the Texas side
six or seven hex ago got me thinkin' Mexico
nobody gonna save my hide

Supermonisticgnostiphistic

Henry lived in penury
addicted to discussions of the fall
a sage and a Pelagian
he refused the postlapsarian gestalt
enabled at the table by a self-effacing shrew
who ranted at and ridiculed his positivist view
he burnt down the proscenium
with *Sterno* and a perfect match for you

Horace thought to bore us
with the details of his misanthropic youth
though quite adept he'd overstepped
the limits of what passes for the truth
with Catullus in his pocket he's a formidable force
who saddles up and rides the atavistic Trojan Horse
he feeds it on your nightmares and he
waters it with women's tears, of course

how supermonisticgnostiphistic

Ezra always said the only way
we motherfuckers make it through
is take what's left with any heft
misremember most and make it new
he burned through every broadcast
with unmitigated rage
but all his rantings earned him was a 4x6 foot cage,
a bed at St. Elizabeth's, and the
will to write another fucking page

how supermonisticgnostiphistic

Pity the Noose

if I seem a bit baffled
when you see me mount the scaffold
it's just 'cause I've been here before
toes knockin' on the gallows door

and if I seem a bit unconcerned
hang around and witness what I done learned
hangman nervous like he know me
seen me hoochie-coochie on the gallows tree

if you see me hangin' don't you cut me loose
pity the noose

if you catch me strollin'
when everybody else be haulin'
hangman creeping up just behind
slipknot tightened on the dotted line

and if I seem none the worse for wear
laughin' on the scaffold like I just don't care
broke line soaking in the mornin' rain
gone to Mississippi on a midnight train

if you see me grinning from the red caboose
pity the noose

if you hear me singin'
when my hands should be wringin'
graveyard shadows fallin' all around
nothin' in the kitchen but a hungry hound

truck patch done gone fallow
deep well done gone shallow
stir my liquor with a rusty nail
hide my money in the county jail

grease my skillet with the hangman's juice
pity the noose

Can O'Worms

I saw Della with her backdoor fella
hanging little bodies on her petticoat line
full lips flapping like a broken umbrella
one eye on her pistol and the other on mine

talk about a can o' worms
talk about a can o' worms
talk about a can o' worms
talk about a can o' worms now

I saw Shannan with a microwave cannon
up on a Bradley with her visor pulled down
camouflage camisole riding up her tramp stamp
laughing at the bitches she was capping with sound

talk about a can o' worms
talk about a can o' worms
talk about a can o' worms
talk about a can o' worms now

I saw Jeannie drink an apple martini
and lick her little finger with a cocaine smile
a hatchet on the table and a bucket in the kitchen
blood spot staining the linoleum tile

talk about a can o' worms
talk about a can o' worms
talk about a can o' worms
talk about a can o' worms now

Metanoia

now some thoughts on paranoia
viva paranoia
viva paranoia

and I don't mean to annoy ya
don't mean to annoy ya
don't mean to annoy ya

you say there be monsters lurkin'
in my paranoia
in my paranoia

I see unseen forces workin'
that seek to destroy ya
that seek to destroy ya

opposite of paranoia
that's right, metanoia
that's right, metanoia

can you translate metanoia?
it means pure obeisance
it means pure obeisance

what's the Greek for pure obeisance?
that's right, metanoia
that's right, metanoia

I say metanoia equals
sit down, shut your piehole
sit down, shut your piehole

sit down, shut your piehole
pieholes question how the dice roll

Rickshaw Rattletrap

out of the way of the rickshaw rattletrap
rotgut rolling drone
out of the way of the rickshaw rattletrap
get 'em in the free speech zone

out of the way of the rickshaw rattletrap
anybody seen my gun?
out of the way of the rickshaw rattletrap
everybody's on the run

everybody now
kowtow now
feel the rickshaw driver's lash
kowtow now
feel the rickshaw driver's lash

everybody now
kowtow now
feel the rickshaw driver's lash
kowtow now
feel the rickshaw driver's lash

where do you go when the go-to men have gone
gunning for the other side?
back to the woods and the ways of the peckerwood
looking for a place to hide

who do you trust when the trust ain't trustworthy?
trust another hand-picked shield?
pop that pup and the puppet master PING-PONG
plant 'em in the potter's field

everybody now
ring round rue
Mr. Rockefeller's throne
ring round rue
Mr. Rockefeller's throne

everybody now
ring round rue
Mr. Rockefeller's throne
ring round rue
Mr. Rockefeller's throne

sound the source of the outsource schemata
cynical scoundrel scam
money ain't made money's only transferred
back it with a bucket of sham

sound the source of the outsource schemata
cynical scoundrel scam
sell it down the river to the bidder with the backing
'cause your money ain't worth a damn

everybody now
kowtow now
feel the rickshaw driver's lash
kowtow now
feel the rickshaw driver's lash

everybody now kowtow now
feel the rickshaw driver's lash kowtow now
feel the rickshaw driver's lash

harvest all political prisoners'
liver, bone, kidney, spleen
sell them parts to the corporate big shots
trade 'em all for gasoline

harvest all political prisoners'
liver, bone, kidney, hair
sell them parts to the corporate big shots
catch 'em in Tienanmen Square

everybody now
Falun Gong
raise the cannibal victim's hand

Falun Gong
raise the cannibal victim's hand

everybody now
Falun Gong
raise the cannibal victim's hand

kowtow now
feel the rickshaw driver's
rickshaw driver's
rickshaw driver's lash

Ulysses

three cheers for Ulysses
he took Calypso for a ride
three cheers for Ulysses
he took Calypso for a ride

and when he got home to Ithaca
he lay right down by Penelope's side

three cheers for Ulysses
he drank the union back again
three cheers for Ulysses
he drank the union back again

they say he strangled all his angels
and left them to drown in a bottle of gin

three cheers for *Ulysses*
it broke the mold and beat the ban
three cheers for *Ulysses*
it broke the mold and beat the ban

we stood around and watched the moli bloom
then saw her swine become a man

Abraxas

tight-wound perimeters of the cerebellum
nobody ever said it would be easy
so many ask for guidance on this carousel
and then refuse the last best answer on their knees

they come back down from their epiphanies
back home from their last preemptive war
they crawl back home to their lost antiphonies
in the back seat of some half-remembered car

nobody looks at a bed of roses
and says "I just don't understand"
nobody listens to the mute Beethoven
and says "I just don't get it, man"

so don't tell me what it's all about now
say instead what it might suggest
let it fire, keep it elemental
all that it means is that everybody's had a guess

Abraxas
Abraxas

so many times I've stripped and tumbled
heard the whimper at the edge of BANG
always spoke when I should have mumbled
always sung when I should have sang

now every cup of coffee is the blood of Jesus
and all those carbon footprints feed the trees
nothing lives forever but it won't die forever either
so just relax now dog, enjoy your fleas

I only ever speak in tongues now
I wrangle serpents because they rankle me
I do sleep well in the arms of the dragon
blind drunk on poison with the will to see

VOCATUS ATQUE NON VOCATUS DEUS
ADERIT (and *c'est la guerre*)
poiesis come and break mimesis
tu est mon semblable et mon frere

Abraxas
Abraxas

Aranzazu

Aranzazu
you there in the briars
the hounds pursue me
and I'm redolent of fire
the sand in my shoes
has made a desert of my dancing
turned my tongue to a fuse
igniting all of which I can't sing

Aranzazu
I want to be your hero
but sorrow intrudes
delivers absolutely zero
every champ has a wound
some obligatory failure
that though sadly attuned
can make a savior of a jailer

Aranzazu
in the thorns of my own making
disheartened and blue
but untouched by promise-breaking
I stand before you
in the wake of insurrection
while fidelity's tomb
opens wide with resurrection

Money Shot Man

yes it's true
the wrecking crew
been working overtime to deconstruct you

and if it's all the same
you played their game
the cash in one hand in the other the flame

and though you've had your fun
it's almost done
I see the count's approaching critical 1

when they start cashing in
on where the pressure's been
be only one dude to usher on in

call him the money shot man
he aim to please and he can
he can't get enough
and he don't need no fluffer, no ma'am

sho 'nuff
you tough
and things all over are increasingly rough

but when they took your soul
they changed the way that you roll
they kept you dealin' while the rest of us fold

and now the fix is in
a pound of flesh for the win
and now the hardest sell's about to begin

I see you've bloomed like a rose
you've even curled back your toes
here come the dude to bring that all to a close

call him the money shot man
he aim to please and he can
he can't get enough
and he don't need no fluffer, no ma'am

call him the money shot man
call him the money shot man
call him the money shot man

Fake This One

you telling me I've overstepped my bounds
I done jumped too high for comfort
and should come back down
I done scared all the horses with the things that I've done
I been feeling way too real better fake this one

fake this one
faithless one

authenticity has overruled
my propensity for being fooled
so now I'm in it just to have me some fun
Jesus take the wheel gonna fake this one

fake this one
faithless one

all them times that I could hardly move
you had me going through the motions,
so you'd just approve
now I'm kinetic as a loaded gun
better ease on off the hammer while I fake this one

fake this one
faithless one

inconvenient as an unplanned kid
more unwelcome than a coffin lid
uninvited as the prodigal son
but obliged if you'll applaud me as I fake this one

fake this one
faithless one
fake this one

Duende

coming straight from the deep Euphrates
Orfeo's gift from the realm of Hades
don't look back baby take his hand
gonna lead us all to the promised land

with do, do, do, duende
do, do do, duende

it seeds the plains of Andalusia
with the bread & wine seeks to infuse you
with the breath of bulls and Eurydice's cry
in the groves of the olive where the spirit is high

on do, do, do, duende
do, do, do, duende

Ignacio lies bleeding in the dust of Alhambra
his ears full of tears and cicada-song-stained skies
the dead possess insects and lizards as they slither
towards the sibyl of San Andres where the lyrics grow
like vines

sing like a serpent in the venomous night
sing for Llorona, she's the woman in white
get your *grito* thrumming like a thaumatrope's wire
a fission in the vision set the demon on fire

with do, do, do, duende
do, do, do, duende

Weedeye

we don't have to do-si-do
we already high
we don't have to *que pasó*
we already fly

we don't have to tap a keg
break or shake or fake a leg
we don't have to bum or beg
we already buy

we don't have to sigh or sing
or slay Goliath with a sling
we don't have to anything
'cept live till we die

now let me think about it:
mushroom tea and a razor blade
I'm diggin' all the way to China
with a luminous spade

cup o' mushroom tea and a razor blade
I'm goin' down to Mississippi 'cause I gotta get paid

we don't have to X or Z
we already Y
we don't have to fricassee
we already fry

we don't have to *parlez vous*
sprechen Sie, hanashimasu
we don't have to tell you true
we already lie

we don't have to queen or king
some extra-circumstantial fling
we don't have to anything
'cept live till we die

well let me think about it:
mushroom tea and a razor blade
and then it's all the way to Baltimore
on premium grade

a cup o' mushroom tea and a razor blade
and then it's down to Yazoo City 'cause I gotta get laid

hands up!
palms out!
I'm under the gun
hands up!
palms out!
it shouldn't be this fun

you hear me talkin' to you?

hands up!

we don't have to white or wheat
we already rye
we don't have to take a seat
we already shy

we don't need no gunny sack
there ain't too much that we don't lack
we all live in one Cadillac
we all of us drive

we don't have to cleave or cling
to the rock of ages suffering
we don't have to anything
'cept live till we die

live till we die
live till we die

A Message from Firmin Desloge

send me up my pocket flask
and blackball Esposito
use my Old Testament
to smash that damned mosquito

for the love of Jesus
put that pistol with my socks
sundown is all I keep
in this here window box

let me fucking sleep on it
I shit you not my friend
keep playing blind man's bluff
till Monday morning ends

everybody tells me
learning shorthand is a bitch
I can pull off anything
that comes without a hitch

at Firmin Desloge
at Firmin Desloge
at Firmin Desloge
at Firmin Desloge

hail, hail, hail Mary
hail the gang's all here
are there any games on tonight?
is there any beer?

long as I got TV
I don't need no second sight
long as I am full of grace
I can't be full of shite

at Firmin Desloge

You Be the Mountain (I'll Be Mohammad)

prophecy depends upon the powers of persuasion
the future's never forecast,
it's made by those who believe
horoscopes and holy tropes may serve well on occasion
but by default they all result in man-made destiny

we bring the fortune closer to ourselves

you be the mountain
I'll be Mohammad
come to me

Nostradamus, Edgar Cayce, Oracle at Delphi
each one had a vision and a loyal retinue
but what if all their followers had never known the self I
take for granted when it comes to winning over you

I'll bring your fortune closer to myself

you be the mountain
I'll be Mohammad
come to me

philosophy is language as bewitchment of the senses
masquerading and parading as some valid means
prophecy is simply love of knowledge's defenses
unrevealed and concealed there behind the scenes

we bring the forces nearer to ourselves

you be the mountain
I'll be Mohammad
come to me

Keels Be Damned

last night I took the plunge
        and slept a mile in your shoes
but I can't take the heat
        for what you're losing while you snooze
April went out with the garbage,
        May came dressed in lies
1984 called it wants back both blinded eyes

I'm coughing bullshit through my fist
crossing fables off my list
I turn the tables and resist
the razor's edge again my wrist

the ship of state has locked its rudders in a tailspin
        let the keels be damned
                set the sails to wind

if you believe the snipe hunt ended badly for the snipe
and have no strong desire
        to ask for proof of rumored tripe
I have seaside land I'll sell for pennies on the pound
it's out in Arizona, you can sail the whole year round

while coughing bullshit through your fist
crossing fables off your list
you'll turn the tables and resist
the razor's edge against your wrist

the fourth estate has slashed its price on unabashed spin
        let the deals go down
                let the sale begin

so call me doubting Thomas 'cause I'll not be satisfied
till I'm allowed to slip my fucking finger in its side
I just can't see what's mad
        in asking proof of what we're told
so I'll be hanging here
        with minds that cannot be controlled

and coughing bullshit through my fist
crossing fables off my list
I turn the tables and resist
the razor's edge again my wrist

the ship of state has locked its rudders in a tailspin
      let the keels be damned
            set the sails to wind

Cain

all I'm gonna answer when you ask me if I'm able
is Cain Cain Cain
if you take a chance or take the mask out of the fable
it's the same same same

no crutch no cross no crook appears
to keep my cranium from crashing defeat
so if I'm walking on the water
or I'm talking to your daughter
it's the Cain that keeps me on my feet

all I'm gonna answer when you ask me if I'm able
is Cain Cain Cain
I'll steal every glance or pawn the warning off the label
for my gain gain gain

no shirt no shoes no shackles man
to keep my shushes all from crying out loud
so if I'm casing up the garden
or I'm facing down the warden
it's the Cain that keeps my head in the clouds

all I'm gonna answer when you ask me if I'm able
is Cain Cain Cain
I can't afford the motion
or the dancer on the table
but I'm payin' payin' payin'

crutch cross crook
peer crane crash feet
feel bold world cold

it's the Cain that keeps me on my feet

Shake the Vine

moonshine gallon o' wine
        follow me down to K-MO
shuffle about in a Chevy DeVille
        as the shadows give way to the dayglow
neon sign looking so fine
        baby's in black with her payload
shake the vine baby's all mine
        honey the wicked are haloed

cuttin' a rug & you're cute as a bug
        & the smoke & the sweat & the fais do
pompadour grease on the floor
        slip on the spot and you're laid O
U T now beauty my wow
        sweepin' you back on your tiptoes
up your feet right on the beat
        killin' me with your stilettos

lie dreaming my spent rebel paramour
        sweet little swindler of my gaze
parked now but a stone's throw
        from the levy near the bottom
where the Odd Fellow's boneyard
        sprawls in cemetery maze

somebody jimmied the dead bolt
        on the icehouse cellar door
and now light from the coal bin
        floods the corners of your eyes
how did we get from the punk to the plenary?
        and where baby where
do we hide all these misbegotten sighs?

fuck-me pumps smackin' your rump
        keepin' me chasin' your tail-o
right behind out of my mind
        doin' my time in your jail-o

you've hidden the keys no early release
                and nothin' for good behavior
life in bars life in cars
                and guilty 'cause I'll never save you.

Holla Petunia

holla petunia with your rope-a-dope spine
later than soon-ya if your mama don't mind
shockin' the fragrants as they drinking their wine
rockin' the vagrance every bit o' so fine

waller petunia in the groove of my bed
slakin' the furrow with the cantaloupe head
cardio caiman with the Cadillac style
you got me harder than math I need the vertical smile

follow petunia if the kitty can't wait
sholla the junior needs a helpin' o' spate
it's got the head of a house cat
and it's caught in the pound
I need to slip you the rib cage of a hungry hound

you the be the pink suncatcher
with the lemonade halo
I'll be your king bee buzzin'
with your pollenator payload

follow petunia if the kitty can't wait
sholla the junior needs a helpin' o' spate
it's got the head of a house cat
and it's caught in the pound
I need to slip you the rib cage of a hungry hound

Éminence Gris Gris

he coming down Bourbon
he struttin' all the way to Marigny
he got a cane and a turban
a little juju for the enemy

he got a sack full of mojo
a John the Conquer root, a marigold
he got a friend in Coco Robichaux
the Loup Garou and the cat bone

he the Éminence Gris Gris
he come gunnin' for the faux

all the bucks in the Vieux Carré
start to scatter when they see The Gray
he may be old but he ain't in the way
at least he's moving though it's slow

the petunias by the back doors
put powdered sugar on their jellyrolls
they feed him chickens that he eats whole
they feed him wishin' he would stay

but he the Éminence Gris Gris
he come gunnin' for the faux

he got a .44 hog leg
straight razor with a dirty blade
I seen him cross himself sideways
when he crossed Esplanade

and now he struttin' to the beat y'all
he makin' thunder with his footfall
ain't nothing secret 'bout the end y'all
no need to wonder 'cause you know

that he the Éminence Gris Gris
he come gunnin' for the faux

I Spit You Out

there is so much more that does not depend
on any thought produced in fields furrowed
by the head's bright plowshare dulled to its own end
by the digger's spiteful spade out-thoroughed

those intent on making names despair
those intent on making waves surrender
all you intent on making fortunes bear
on every cryptomnesic lender

I spit you out into the lukewarm billabong
I spit you mingling in the wide arroyo
I spit you back into the sea arm's come-along
I spit you up into the winding oxbow

there is so much more that does not depend
on any brief and inadvertent moment
the sparrow exits the storm it cannot amend
and for a spark finds rest from winter's torment

those intent on educating fools beware
those intent on splitting hairs remember
all your misspent time debating rules we fear
has rent your divinatory shine asunder

I spit you out into the lukewarm billabong
I spit you mingling in the wide arroyo
I spit you back into the sea arm's come-along
I spit you up into the winding oxbow

there is so much more that does not depend
on any theory sold as truth's dominion
your books your science inch forth quite hesitant
they are nothing more than merely frank opinion

those intent on desecrating graves you share
with those intent on battling by the hymns' direction

those intent on claiming bravery wears
some hallowed smile are yourselves infection

I spit you out into the lukewarm billabong
I spit you mingling in the wide arroyo
I spit you back into the sea arm's come-along
I spit you up into the winding oxbow

Drapetomaniac

you wear them shackles on your guns
but you can't break your cage and run
you better
drop it
drop it
drop it
you drapetomaniac

we hear the clanking of your chains
we hear the wheels turn in your brains
you better
drop it
drop it
drop it
you drapetomaniac

there'll be no row the boat ashore
be no knuckles at your door
no freedom train to ride
till they refuel

there'll be no comfort and no cheer
be no sympathetic ear
for the words you speak
are the ravings
of a fool

you'll have no friends you'll have no fear
we'll keep you safe, we'll keep you here
you better
drop it
drop it
drop it
you drapetomaniac

Hystery Train

there ain't no mystery 'bout this train
been circlin' the drain
long since it come ramblin' down

tracks all but forgotten
railroad ties all rotten

blind engineer's mind unsound

locked up in a boxcar
washed up like a rock star
singin' someone else's lines

like determination
beats predestination's
the game I play to pass the time

ain't no mystery 'bout this train
been negative in gain
long since it come shamblin' round

switchmen they all insane
tickets they all one way
all of us know where it's bound

vows all but unbroken
lines all but unspoken
watch as the world passes by

we stagger down the gangway
smilin' as the train sways
rollin' through this endless lie

Chemtrailer Trash

I tattoo the sky with alchemy
in my TAKAMO jalopy
I ain't your barium enemy
baby call me your chemo sabe

I can slick back the clouds like angel hair
from Nome down to Landover
I can tune your HAARP and keep looking sharp
and give the ozone hole a comb-over

'cause I'm chemtrailer trash
chemtrailer trash
chemtrailer trash
and I'm coming to your neighborhood

33 19 17 baby stuck up on my nosecone
while an old friend trudges
to the beat of his judges
I pick up his torch and I run

so your corn needs aluminum siding
I can do the job in a sonic boom
I'm a miracle worker, a crop circle jerker
a witch on a strontium broom

and I'm chemtrailer trash
chemtrailer trash
chemtrailer trash
and I'm moving to your neighborhood
now

Triptych

I came fourth but I was born to run
so to set my course as the seventh son
I split my wealth by means of stealth
and I made a triptych of myself
I made a triptych of myself

panel the first is the least of the cursed
not the worst of the best or the best of the worst
like the good thief hanging next to Jesus Christ
it's got a one-way ticket bound for paradise

I came fourth but I was born to run
so to set my course as the seventh son
I split my wealth by means of stealth
and I made a triptych of myself
I made a triptych of myself

the pane on the left is the panel bereft
what it took to its heart it acquired by theft
it's a soul less limits with a powerful thirst
for the venomous toxin of the world it reversed

I came fourth but I was born to run
so to set my course as the seventh son
I split my wealth by means of stealth
and I made a triptych of myself
I made a triptych of myself

panel the third is the undeclared word
it's a numinous sign and though luminous, blurred
It's the anchor that dangles in its triplicate views
but it was forged in the fires at the end of the fuse

I came fourth but I was born to run
so to set my course as the seventh son
I split my wealth by means of stealth
and I made a triptych of myself
I made a triptych of myself

AFTERWARD:

One
FOR THE MEMORIES

mem[ory]sahib

I wish memory would often not serve me,
that it would pick up the phone and call in sick,
or hum Johnny Paycheck under its breath while it
went about its business of dogging my every move.

I wish it would take long, tee-mar-two-nee lunches,
talk shit about the boss with the other small minds,
come back drunk to work and go home whenever it
good-&-goddamned pleased. I wish it would stay there.

I wish at best it would punch the clock an hour late
and leave forgotten memos on its ever unkempt desk.
I wish it would misquote me and make shit up because
it never got things right. Wish it wouldn't work for free.

I wish memory would never serve me again, that
it would pick up the torch & pitchfork and storm
the crystal palace of my clear & present mind.
I wish it would say it needs me like a bullet in the brain.

I wish it weren't such a gossip and more analogous to a
steel mousetrap—if it can't be not inclusive then at least
be more selective. I wish it would lie when I write I
wish I could remember why I ever thought to write this.

Notes

[p.1]
In Tex-Mex slang, a Tocayo is a person who shares the same given name as that of another. There are several theories about the origin of the word including the following two which I find to be the most convincing: A) That the word comes from the Nahuatl *tocaitl* meaning "nickname" or "fame" (the implication of the latter being that in Nahuatl society—as in most societies—many children were named in honor of distinguished, or famous individuals; B) That it comes from the ancient Roman wedding ritual in which the bride would turn to the groom and, in asking that his name be given to her, would say "*Ubi tu Gaius, ego Gaia*" ("Whereas you gain (me), I gain (you)").

In the case of the latter, the meaning of the words goes beyond simple name-sharing; it implies a bond of metaphysical proportions. The Romans believed that by speaking the words "*Ubi tu Gaius, ego Gaia*" during a wedding ceremony, husband and wife became two parts of the same person. In Spanish, the Latin words are pronounced phonetically "*Ubi tu cayo, ego caya*." The theory is that the entire phrase has been contracted to the simple "tu cayo," or "tocayo," and has evolved in the present to mean simply that two people share the same name; though the original, deeper bond is often implied.

[p.48 (Anagram: 'Sonnet 18').]
Taking the techniques used in *Multiverse*, a book by my friend and fellow poet Mike Smith, as inspiration, I used every letter from Shakespeare's "Sonnet 18" to craft this anagrammatic poem. With the exception of only a few unavoidable prepositions and articles, I have only repeated two words: "every" and "hath."

[pp.103–42.]
All of the selections in *Unaccompanied* are lyrics written for Churchwood, the avant blues-rock quintet for and in which I have been writing and performing since 2007. To date, Churchwood has released three studio LPs and an EP on the Saustex Media label of San Antonio, TX. To learn more about Churchwood, visit the band's pages on Facebook, Reverbnation, Myspace, and/or Wikipedia.

[p.121.]
From the Sabine River to the Rio Grande, Texas meets the Gulf of Mexico along 367 miles of coastline and more than 3,300 miles of bay shores. At about the halfway point between the Sabine and the Rio Grande lie Aransas Pass, Aransas Bay, and Port Aransas. All three are part of a region explored as early as 1519 by the Spanish explorer Alonzo Álvarez De Pineda.

By 1718, emissaries of Spain had mapped the area which was settled by Spanish and French immigrants not long thereafter. In 1750, a Spanish fort was established at the northern end of Live Oak Point near the present-day bridge that links the towns of Fulton and Lamar. The Spanish called it *Fortaleza Aranzazu* (Fort Aranzazu) after the "Santuario de Arantzazu," a Franciscan sanctuary located in Oñati, Basque Country, Spain.

Legend has it that the sanctuary earned its named after the Virgin Mary appeared to a Basque shepherd named Rodrigo de Balanzategui in 1468. Balanzategui claimed that the Virgin stood surrounded by impenetrable, razor-sharp thorn bushes. The apparition so startled Balanzategui that he shouted "Arantzan zu?!" ("You, among the thorns?!").

According to the etymological explanation, the original place name stems from "arantza + zu," and means "place abounding in hawthorn." Balanzategui's exclamation, through linguistic corruption, first became *Arantzazu* in Spanish, then Aranzazu along the thorny, cactus-covered Texas coast, and has since settled into the current Tex-Mex locution as *Aransas*. My wife Mary and I have spent a lot of miraculous time on the Texas coast either in or near Port Aransas. 'Aranzazu' is for her.

[p. 141]
The musical version of this poem includes a bridge with lyrics by Julien Peterson:

"dig dig dig in that dirt
pull pull pull at them weeds
swat swat swat at them flies
scrape scrape scrape your rough knees".

Acknowledgments

I'd like to thank the many friends without whom this collection would not have been possible: John Matthias for his enduring patience, guidance, and advice; Tony Frazer for his support, the opportunity to publish again, and for breathing new life into the selected poems found in this edition; Jeff Smith of Saustex Media for providing the many lyrics in this collection their first and most memorable setting, not to mention a permanent home for them in San Antonio; Jon Langford for his gift of good gab and the brilliant cover art; George Brainard for the author's photograph; and my fellow members of Churchwood: Bill Anderson, Adam Kahan, Billysteve Korpi, and Julien Peterson for their friendship, good music, and the inspiration for many of the words in this book. I'd like also to acknowledge my family, especially my father, whose enduring support of my passions has never flagged. And last, but certainly never least, I want to thank my wife Mary Cat, in whose inability to doubt I take refuge, and in whose fierce belief in and devotion to me, a man who sometimes deserves neither, I find the supreme example of fin'amor.

Some of the poems here were previously published in the following journals:

'Tocayo,' first appeared in *The Notre Dame Review* #28 (Summer/Fall 2009).
'The Catch,' first appeared in *The Notre Dame Review* #21 (Winter 2006).
'While you're out remember,' first appeared in *Stand*, Vol. 6 (1) (Spring 2005).
'The Kings of Cryptomnesia,' first appeared in *Stand*, Vol. 9 (4) (Spring 2010).
'Diptych: Drapetomania,' first appeared in *Fifth Wednesday Journal*, Issue 8 (Spring 2011).
Selections from 'The Cottage Wall' first appeared as 'Six Poems' in *Stand*, Vol. 14 (2) (Spring 2016).
'Thou Philip, Thief of Loco-Focos,' first appeared in *PN Review*, Vol. 23, No. 6 (July/August 1997).
'St. Louis Gothic,' first appeared in *Stand*, Vol. 9 (4) (Spring 2010).
'Sestina: Querencia,' first appeared in *Stand*, Vol. 9 (4) (Spring 2010).
'In Nomine Something,' first appeared in *Stand*, Vol. 9 (4) (Spring 2010).
'To the Dryad in Her Eightieth Year,' fist appeared in *Stand*, Vol. 9 (4) (Spring 2010).
'Il Faut Aller Voir,' first appeared in *The Notre Dame Review* #28 (Summer/Fall 2009).
'F U T H A R K 2K,' was first published in its entirety in *The Possibility of Language: Seven New Poets*, ed. Jeffrey Roessner, (Lake Forest: Samizdat Editions, 2001).
'Why the Earth Shakes,' 'A Handful of Dust,' and 'Mythissippi Mud' first appeared in *Samizdat* No. 2 (Winter 1999).
'Thumbnails for a Portrait of Sacher-Masoch' first appeared in *Dànta: Journeys in Poetry* No. 1 (Summer 2002).

'Sestina for the Birds' first appeared in *PN Review*, Vol. 23, No. 6 (July/August 1997).

The following lyrics were first published by Saustex Songs—BMI:

from the LP *Churchwood* (2011):
Pontiac Flanagan
Rimbaud Diddley
Vendidi Fumar
Melungeon in the Dungeon
Supermonisticgnostiphistic
Pity the Noose
Can O'Worms
Ulysses
Abraxas

from the EP *Churchwood: Just the Two of Us* (2012):
Metanoia
Rickshaw Rattletrap

from the LP *Churchwood 2* (2013):
Aranzazu
Money Shot Man
Fake This One
Duende
Weedeye
A Message from Fermin Desloge
You Be the Mountain (I'll Be Mohammad)
Keels Be Damned

from the LP *Churchwood 3: Trickgnosis* (2014):
Cain
Shake the Vine
Holla Petunia
Éminence Gris Gris
I Spit You Out
Drapetomaniac
Hystery Train
Chemtrailer Trash
Triptych

CPSIA information can be obtained
at www.ICGtesting.com
Printed in the USA
FSOW01n0429101216
28219FS